Samuel Wilberforce

Heroes of Hebrew History

Samuel Wilberforce

Heroes of Hebrew History

ISBN/EAN: 9783337189136

Printed in Europe, USA, Canada, Australia, Japan

Cover: Foto ©ninafisch / pixelio.de

More available books at **www.hansebooks.com**

HEROES OF HEBREW HISTORY

BY

SAMUEL WILBERFORCE, D.D.

BISHOP OF WINCHESTER

NEW EDITION

LONDON
W. H. ALLEN AND CO., 13, WATERLOO PLACE, S.W.
1890

THE following sketches, with the exception of "David the King," have already appeared in the pages of *Good Words*. They are now republished at the request of many who desire to possess them in a separate form.

May God's blessing make them useful!

S. W.

WINCHESTER HOUSE,
    Feb., 1870.

CONTENTS.

		PAGE
ABRAHAM	. . . . . .	1
JACOB	. . . . . .	30
JOSEPH	. . . . . .	57
MOSES	. . . . . .	92
JOSHUA	. . . . . .	131
SAMSON THE JUDGE	. . .	161
SAMUEL THE PROPHET	. . .	198
DAVID THE KING	. . . .	229
THE MAN OF GOD WHO CAME OUT OF JUDAH	.	264
MICAIAH, THE SON OF IMLA	. . .	294
ELIJAH	. . . . . .	318
ELISHA	. . . . . .	341

ABRAHAM.

HERE is the fountain-head of Hebrew hero-life—the time when Abram was born in the house of his father Terah. Here we stand amongst the great progenitors of our race. Abram's birth was but two hundred and eighty years after the flood: a shorter period than has passed since Queen Elizabeth sat under a tree which is still alive in Hatfield Park, and saw the approach of the royal messenger who brought her, instead of the expected warrant to a dungeon and a scaffold, the tidings of her succession to the throne of England.

Noah lived, according to the reckonings of chronology as probable as any, for sixty-two years after the birth of Abram, and may well have repeated in his hearing the wonderful story of that rescued life which the hand of God Himself had shut for safety into the ark of gopher-wood. It may be that by such communings was first nourished in the soul of the patriarch that supreme trust in God's presence with him and care for him which was the warp into which was worked the great spiritual life of the friend of Jehovah and the father of the faithful. He was born to Terah in Ur of the Chaldees, one of the cities of the rich plain of Shinar, into which flowed the first streams of the life of the repeopled world—the cradle of the first Babylonish empire of which, through the mists of the long ages, we may dimly see the shadowy form of the great Nimrod, the "mighty hunter before the Lord," laying the colossal foundations. Thus though himself of the favoured race of Shem, Terah, the father of Abram, lived in the midst of the first Hamitic empire. This dwelling in the tents of Ham gives a certain probability to the stories which Arabian and Jewish traditions have woven round his name. Holy Scripture tells us only, with its wonted simplicity of narrative, that "Terah dwelt on the other side of the flood" (the characteristic name of "the great river, the river Euphrates") "in old time, and served other gods" (Josh. xxiv. 2).

But the story grows in other records. Terah is a maker as well as a worshipper of idols. He is high in favour with the mighty Nimrod, and a chief captain in the Hamitic host. Abram, his son, is a believer in the unity of the Godhead; keeping alive, under the secret visitations of grace, the true tradition of the faith as it had been received from Noah. In the fervour of his spirit he destroys his father's idols, who accuses him to Nimrod. Then the grand drama which was acted generations after in the days of Nebuchadnezzar so gloriously on the plain of Dura by the three descendants of the patriarch is asserted to have been anticipated by their great ancestor, on the plain of Shinar. Abram refuses the offers of the idolaters, and is cast into a burning furnace, from which Jehovah delivers him unharmed. Some striking differences of narrative seem to contradict the idea of the story being a mere casting back of later history into a fabulous antiquity. For instead of the constant fidelity of the three Jewish worthies, it is said in the old record of Abram's trial that Haran, Abram's brother, was sitting by and saying in his heart, "If Abram overcomes, I am on his side; and if Nimrod overcomes, I am on his." So when Abram was delivered, they turned to Haran, and demanded, "On whose side art thou?" and, seeing that Abram was safe, he answered, "I am of Abram's." So they cast him too into the furnace. But his heart not being whole with God, there was no deliverance for him, and so he was consumed.

These old traditions may or may not hold in solution facts historically true. They may be nothing more than the nimbus glory which streams from great saints and manifests itself to us by lighting up into an encircling crown the floating atoms of the past. But whether they record facts or imaginations, we know that dealings of God with his faithful servant not less wonderful than these did mark the life of Abram in that old plain of Shinar. So much the words of inspiration tell us: "The God of glory appeared unto our father Abraham when he was in Mesopotamia, before he dwelt in Charran, and said, Get thee out of thy country and from thy kindred, and come into the land that I shall show thee" (Acts vii. 2, 3).

Such was the summons, and the obedience of Abram was immediate and complete. The traditions of a life were broken up, he went forth out of Ur of the Chaldees, not knowing whither he went" (Heb. xi. 8). The bitterness of that first parting with kinsmen and relatives and accustomed scenes and the habits of a life was mercifully lessened by his aged father Terah's going forth with him into the unknown land. How the old man was moved to this migration we can but guess. Nahor, the eldest son of the house, was dead: and though Haran, the second brother, remained at Ur, yet it may well be that Terah saw in the character of Abram that which marked him out as the foremost of his family, and therefore clung to the mysterious fortunes of his youngest son. And so they journeyed, as men journeyed in those days of old, with sons and daughters, and shepherds, and man-servants and maid-servants, and goods, across the roadless steppes, by the tracks which other travellers had marked upon the great plain. At Charran, in Mesopotamia, the cloudy pillar of God's presence halted, and for a while the migration stayed. There for Terah's lifetime they abode; understanding, however, as it seems, that this was but a broken halt, and that the more distinct summons of the original command beckoned him yet farther. And so, when Terah's bones were laid in their resting-place, the march again began, and upon a grander scale. As yet, though parted from their early home, the wanderers had not altogether quitted the land of their nativity. That patriarchal realm was bounded by the mighty Euphrates—the "great river," "the flood;" the "other side" of which to those ancient men was little less of a partition from all they knew of life than were the waters of the great Atlantic to the adventurous Columbus. Right across the flood the mystic summons called the son of Terah, and over it he dutifully sped, and came into the land of Canaan.

This second migration is marked as the turning-point of his life—the first great venture of his faith. The former migration had been one of those tribe movements which appertained to the early history of man, when from the East, in which he had been cradled, he moved forward, as the tides of ocean sway under the moon, "to replenish the earth and possess it." Then, his father, Terah, is spoken of as "having taken Abram, and they went forth from Ur of the Chaldees;" but now the patriarch goes forth alone; now the Voice calls him, and he follows. "The Lord had said unto Abram, Get thee out of thy country and from thy kindred, and from thy father's house, unto a land that I will show thee. . . . . So Abram departed as the Lord had spoken unto him. . . . . And Abram was seventy and five years old when he departed out of Haran."

On the whole face of the replenishing earth such another sight was nowhere to be seen. It was the single grand spectacle of humanity on which angels gazed with wondering joy. He was perhaps then the sole type of that one true

Man who in the after-ages should spring from his seed to do the Will of God perfectly; to hear always that voice, and always to follow it. This nobleness, different indeed in measure, but in kind the same, the faith of Abram imparted to his soul. He rose above this earth because he believed simply in God. This is the record of the Highest. When Abram was ninety years old and nine, "the Lord appeared and said unto him, Walk before me, and be thou perfect." This was the one grandeur of his life; and this was to be for ever commemorated in the new name given to him. "Neither shall thy name be any more Abram" ("father of elevation"), "but thy name shall be Abraham" ("father of a multitude"). This walking before God it was which invested him with that glorious character which the voice of the Lord himself, when speaking to Abimelech, attributed to him. "He is a prophet, and he shall pray for thee, and thou shalt live" (Gen. xx. 7). We never read of Abraham's predicting the future, and yet he was, for the voice of God declared it, "a prophet."

It is full of instruction for us to see wherein his

prophetic character consisted. For we shall have poor and unworthy conceptions concerning the mighty office of the prophets of Jehovah so long as we confound them with the tribe of the mere predictors of the future. Such a prescience was indeed often imparted to the prophet to qualify him for his office. But, first, it was the accident, not the essence of his office. In the soothsayer and the oracle priestess, on the contrary, that declaration of the future, real or pretended, by guess or enigma, by dark sign or darker word, was the very central point of the whole ministration. Men came in the hope of having the blinding curtain which hung over the future lifted up for them; they sought nothing else; they could receive nothing more. But so it was not with the prophet of Jehovah. He was the witness to man of the living God of righteousness and truth. If he did predict, he did it to shake some ungodly heart with terror, or to build up some faithful soul in hope. Abram, though, so far as we know, he uttered no predictions, was a grand fulfiller of this office. By his simple obedience and his glorious faith he bore a witness to Jehovah such as no other man then living, perhaps as no other mere man through all the generations of the sons of Adam, ever equalled. As, with all belonging to him, he crossed the flood, going he knew not whither, at the bidding of the Voice, how grandly did he mirror back to all times and all ages the faithfulness and truth of Him in whom he so trusted! Thus in this central characteristic of the prophetic office Abraham ranks high in the goodly fellowship.

But, again, the prophet of Jehovah differs from the soothsayers in this essential feature of his predictive faculty. The mere oracular utterance declared, or professed to declare, some isolated and disjointed fact, foreseen in itself by some accidental prescience, as the eye may see some solitary star through a chance opening in the cloudy canopy which veils the general heavens. Instead of this, the true prophet's revelation of the future based itself on the present and on the past. On the present, because to him who believes in the righteous government of the all-good and the unchangeable the present is ever full of types of the future, which, until they are fulfilled all remain dark to common eyes, but which are opened to the reading of his instructed gaze; and on the past, because that past as it lies written in history is but the record of God's dealings heretofore with man; and it is the ever-unfolding line of God's dealings which is opened to him. The law and the right of the moral government of the mighty King, not the unmeaning triviality of some separate event which an idle or an interested curiosity longs to foreknow, is that which it is given to him to discern. To him therefore the past is the future, as that future lies yet folded up and waiting for its development within the germinating seed; and to him therefore prophecy is history prolonged. His prediction, whether in word or in act, is the utterance of his spirit, as under the teaching of the Spirit of Jehovah it reaches forth into that yet future development of the truth and right with which it now commerces in God.

Now, such a gift of prophecy as this was most surely given to Abraham. For Christ has said, " Abraham desired to see my day, and he saw it and was glad." The great insight of his faith reached on so far as that. When he received as simply true the word of God concerning the birth of Isaac—against hope believing in hope that he might become the father of many nations—not staggering at the promise of God through unbelief, but was strong in faith, giving glory to God, and being fully persuaded that what He had promised He was able to perform, as the God who calleth those things which be not as if they were (Rom. iv. 17—21), then he received the promise of the true Son, in whom all the families of the earth should be blessed. Here we see before our eyes this great insight of the prophet of Jehovah into the typical character of the present; for in this gift of Isaac beyond the rule of nature he read the gift of the virgin-born; in the present son of promise, the coming in the fulness of time of the promised seed; in the son of Sarah, the Son of Mary. It may well be that his eye was opened to read further types which for others lay impenetrably folded up in the blinding present. As he climbed the hill of sacrifice, ready to accomplish that vast venture of his unquestioning faith, may he not have seen in the child of promise, bearing beside him up the steep the wood of the sin-offering, the figure of the child of far greater promise, of the desire, not of his eyes only, but of all nations, as He too bore up the hill of Calvary the wood on which He was to be offered up, the one sacrifice for sin? (Heb. xi. 17—19.) Surely he foresaw the offering of the one sacrifice for sin when he saw the day of Christ and was glad. Nay, may we not gather that even the mighty mystery of the resurrection of the Lord was read by him in the giving back to him of Isaac, from those pregnant words of the Epistle to the Hebrews which tell us that his faith grasped the seemingly audacious hope that "God was able to raise Isaac even from the dead?"

This prophetic gift, then, we may trace in Abraham.

But further, it is the prophet's office not only to read, but also to declare the future. This he may do in word or in act. Ezekiel as truly prophesied in act, when, at God's command he portrayed the city of Jerusalem on a hill, and laid siege against it, and cast a mount against it, and lay on his right side and then on his left side, as when he uttered the predictive words which foretold the coming judgment. And in act, who was a greater prophet than Abraham? His whole life was, in the highest sense of the mysterious word, a prophecy. This leaving Charran, this "crossing of the flood," what else were they but acted prophecies of the mighty truth which shines conspicuously in the Gospel pages, that the man who would inherit the heavenly Canaan must be content to leave father and mother and all that he hath, and to follow houseless and homeless the call of Jesus? And as it was from the beginning, so it was unto the end. Almost every recorded fact in Abraham's life is full of prophecy. In this high sense he is indeed the father of the faithful; and the history of all his children is fore-acted in himself. How simply and emphatically was he in act the true forerunner of all who ever since have "died in faith!" (Heb. xi. 14—16.) Thus it was in the point of his history which we had reached. After the signal obedience which was accomplished in his leaving, at God's call, his home and all that he had, and crossing the Euphrates, to be led on he knew not whither, he is brought to the northern fords of Jordan, and crosses over them into the land of his future inheritance. The district that he entered was the most fertile of that whole valley of abundance. He passed up the valley of the Jabbok into the plain of Moreh. There, when his eye had been filled with the sense of beauty which is so keenly awakened after a weary journey through a waste, by the sight of abundance and verdure, "the Lord appeared unto Abram and said, Unto thy seed will I give this land" (Gen. xii. 7). There, in the fulness of his grateful trust, Abram built his first altar in the land of promise to the God who had appeared unto him. Perhaps he thought that all his wanderings were over, that thenceforward he might know again in this land of beautiful fertility the sweetnesses of home; but it was not to be so. He is indeed allowed to halt for a season in the earthly paradise he had entered. The first taste of the good land was to be one of rest after labour, of enjoyment after suffering, of the springing water and the vine and olive, after the droughty, fruitless, barren desert. But the rest was not to last long, or even his faithful energy might have been relaxed; for "over sweetness breedeth gall, and too much joy, even spiritual, maketh men wanton;"* and so he tastes and passes on. All that he looks upon shall be his; but it is not his yet: "the Canaanite was then in the land." The enemy must be cast out before the joy of the faithful can be full. The time of that deliverance is hidden deep in the unrevealed counsels of God. In Abraham's day the iniquity of the Amorites was not yet full: for all his children in faith the mystery of iniquity is not yet accomplished. Of that day and that hour knoweth no man. But it shall come. Evil shall be driven in upon itself: the seven nations of the wicked shall be driven out. The heir of all things shall possess the earth. And so the rich plain is to be left almost as soon as it has been gained; and from its luxurious ease the guiding pillar leads him on to the safe but barren upland

* Hooker.

There he pitches his tent, "on a mountain on the east of Bethel, having Bethel on the west and Hai on the east;" and there again "he builded an altar unto the Lord, and called on the name of the Lord." Bethel and Hai, names unknown as yet in any sacred story, famous as they shall thereafter become for God's dealings with his people, for God's revelation to his saints. As yet there was no Bethel, no "house of God;" it was known only as the district lying near to Luz, a heathen city of the elder Canaanite possession, the dreary dwelling-place of the godless and the idol worshippers. That first altar to Jehovah, as it rose under the hand of Abram, was itself a prophecy of all that was to follow; it foretold God's gracious vision to the wandering outcast from the family of Isaac; and again God's meeting him, as he came back from Padan-aram, and, after the mysterious night wrestling, endowing him with the name of Israel—that name of mystic significance, whether it be "thou hast contended,"* or, as the elders have it, the "prince with God." † It prophesied of the time

* So Gesenius and Rosenmuller. † St. Jerome.

when the ark of the covenant should here be fixed, with Aaron's grandson ministering before it, and when the repentant children of Israel should come here in their extremity to seek succour and direction from their fathers' God (Judges xx. 18, 31; xxi. 2).

Yet even here, at his mountain encampment, the faithful wanderer was not long to halt. To make his act of prophecy perfect, he was to be as destitute of any fixed habitation as is the Bedouin Arab of the wilderness. "Abram journeyed, going on still towards the south" (Gen. xii. 9). He was to show that he had "embraced the promises of God and confessed that he was a stranger and pilgrim on the earth" (Heb. xi. 13).

Then began those perpetual marches of his consecrated tent wherewith he moved up and down the land which his seed was hereafter to inherit, though not so much was given him in possession as to set his foot upon. And so with some brief, interposed intervals, in which he sojourned in Egypt, or amongst the Philistine lords on the plains which skirted the neighbouring seaboard, his long after-life was spent upon the rocky ridges and high grassy uplands of the hill country of Canaan; on which there slept in the sunlight, or fluttered beneath the sweeping breezes of the night, the white folds of the great wanderer's tent. What a sight it was for the watchers of God's angel host, as they marked the man of faith standing well-nigh alone on a rebellious, unbelieving earth, building from post to post his altar to the Lord, confessing His name, doing His Will, interceding for offenders, communing as a man communes with his friend, with the Almighty Jehovah!

As those sacred circuits measured out the land, attesting its future possession by the faithful, what a prophecy did they utter of the setting up, on the mountain of the Lord of Hosts, of Messiah's kingdom! For within those circling folds there was gathered, in seed and promise, all the future Church of Christ. There was the family in covenant with Jehovah; there, the living faith which from generation to generation joins the soul of man to God There was the only sure knowledge of the one true God; there, the revelation of His Will. There, in the mysterious visitation of the three stranger forms before his tent door, subsiding into the single presence of Jehovah, was already a declaration of the hidden mystery of the Trinity in Unity. There, given perhaps already by sacred tradition from Noah—there, in vision, in dream, and by voice, vouchsafed to the watching patriarch, was all which should grow, under the prophetic breathing of the future, into the lively oracles of God. There, already, faith spread its strong wing, and soared in what were hereafter David's Messianic Psalms, and Isaiah's evangelic predictions. There, in the shadows of the covenant, sealed in circumcision and renewed in burnt-offerings, were the great sacraments of the Gospel Church, waiting only the appointed day of their open manifestation.

Surely, in no other time or place has the earth ever seen a life like that of the hero patriarch, which God's hand had shut within those enfolding curtains. By many a fire of furnace heat that great soul was tempered and annealed to do and bear without reserve the Will of God When, leaving all behind him, he crossed in simple trust the great river, he would, in man's judgment, have been pronounced already perfect in faith. Yet further trial brought to light an unsuspected weakness even in that great heart, and under a wholly new temptation the faith even of the father of the faithful wavered. A famine drove him into Egypt, which was even then beginning to develop its early heathen civilisation, strongly marked with deep lines of sensual indulgence and despotic power. The tented wanderer shrank as the Arab of the desert shrinks from the crowded city life, and he who through his desert migration and mountain wanderings had found ever in those vast solitudes abundant companionship in the presence of his God, felt himself forsaken and alone in the more depressing isolation of being immersed in the full busy stream of a life which was separated in every sympathy from his own. In this depression his great heart sank within him, and he sought to save his life, endangered through the coveted beauty of Sarai, by the denial of his wife. God was better to him than his fears, and delivered him from the danger which he dreaded, and he came up from Egypt enriched by the largess of its king, and safe under the shadow of the Almighty hand.

To purge away this remaining weakness he was still held by the hand of Love in the furnace heat. It was specially in all that concerned the child of promise that the long discipline and perfecting of his faith lay. There was first the long nine-and-twenty years of waiting from the date of the first promise for this still protracted birth. The slow years of waiting crept on until to mere nature the gift seemed to be impossible. Then when Isaac had been given there was the casting forth of Ishmael, who it is plain had greatly engaged the affections of the otherwise childless father. The thing was very grievous in Abraham's sight because of his son (Gen. xxi. 11). Then, so far as Scripture has recorded his life, there was a lull in the sharp discipline of the great patriarch. The early years of Isaac's life passed peacefully, and he grew up in his father's tent, a meek and docile son, from childhood to maturity. But when this one delight of the aged pair, this gift beyond nature, this heir of so many promises, was something more than twenty years of age, once more his father's faith was subjected to the signal trial into which all the lesser ones of his life ran up and found their completion. He is called upon to offer up this beloved son, the one gift of gifts, in sacrifice upon the mountain of Moriah. He hears the voice, and he obeys: slowly up the hill of sacrifice his patient feet climb; the victim bearing the wood for the burnt-offering by his side. His faith is tested to the very uttermost. For not until the sacrificial knife is raised to slay his son is that obedient hand stayed. This was the last great act of his discipline. Now at last his noble, single-hearted faith was perfected. So the voice of God proclaimed: "By myself have I sworn, saith the Lord: for because thou hast done this thing, and hast not withheld thy son, thine only son, that in blessing I will bless thee, and in multiplying I will multiply thy seed as the stars of heaven; .... and in thy seed shall all the nations of the earth be blessed, because thou hast obeyed my voice" (Gen. xxii. 16—18).

The special purpose of the sacred records of the life of Abraham is written plain upon their surface. They are chosen with the one plain purpose of illustrating in this chiefest example the life of faith. They show us its root in the word of Jehovah; its fruit in simple obedience; in the grandeur of an unfaltering trust; in the fulness of a life of sacrifice. They show us its nourishment in secret communings with God, its reward in the gift of righteousness, and with that the promised inheritance of the world.

But whilst the great purpose of the sacred narrative is to show us how this grand faith was formed, perfected, and crowned in Abraham, enough besides this is left on record to exhibit him as a real man and not an imaginary figure. Thus we see him not only in his acts and communings as the friend of God, but also on his earthly side, in his intercourse with his immediate kindred on earth, with those in whose borders he sojourned or with whom the events

of his life brought him into contact. All of
these wear the same character. He is the Great
Shiek. Grand, generous, powerful; when necessary, warlike, and always munificent. Thus
when increasing riches make the parting of himself and Lot, his brother's son, necessary for the
peace of their retainers, he cedes at once to the
younger man the choice of habitation, content
himself to take whichever district is abandoned
to him. His nephew's greedy selection of the
well-watered plain involves him in the calamities
which soon after overwhelmed the native chieftains. One of the many migrations of the more
warlike northern tribes broke upon the rich and
enervated dwellers in the vale of Sodom; and
the retiring wave of plundering aggression bore
back with it, amongst the captives, the kinsman
of Abraham. Though Lot's misfortunes had
been the fruit of his greed, yet the generous
heart of Abraham is at once touched to the
quick by the terrible captivity of his brother's
son. With Bedouin speed Abraham armed
three hundred and eighteen trained men, born
in his service, and with three confederate chiefs,

Aner, Eshcol, and Mamre, attacks the retreating plunderers, routs them completely, rescues his nephew and his goods: and even drives back the emigrating horde into their own distant territory.

The returning conqueror is met by a twofold greeting; one enveloped in no little mystery; both displaying highly indicative traits of Abraham's character. To the king of Sodom's proposition, that he should yield to him the ransomed captives and retain the recovered goods, Abraham's answer reveals at once his estimate of that evil brood, in the midst of whom Lot from covetousness had so rashly settled, and his jealousy for the honour of his God. "I have lift up mine hand unto the most high God, the possessor of heaven and earth, that I will not take from a thread to a shoe latchet, and that I will not take anything that is thine, lest thou shouldest say, I have made Abram rich" (Gen. xiv. 22, 23).

The other greeting was from that half-revealed figure which reappears with undiminished mystery in the Epistle to the Hebrews. Who this Melchizedek was—the king of Salem, the priest of the most high God, the king of peace to whom Abram gave tithes of all—conjecture has from the earliest Christian time been busy to discover. The older belief rejected as impossible the newest theory that he was a Canaanitish prince, and delighted to see under this garb of mystery the priestly son of Noah, the venerable Shem, transported by the might of his God to bless his great descendant in whom now the whole line of the faithful was embodied.

The burial of Sarah throws out again into a strong relief the figure of the patriarch as he shows amidst the men around him. His first and only possession of the land of Canaan is the cave of Machpelah, which he purchases of Ephron the Hittite, that he may lay in it the body of the dead wife, who through so many eventful years had been the faithful sharer of his ventures and his wanderings, and whom God himself had changed from being Sarai the quarrelsome, into Sarah the princess.

The aged man comes with his precious burden to mourn for Sarah and to weep for her. "I am a stranger," he says, in a half-deprecating tone, to the children of Heth, "and a sojourner with you: give me a possession of a burying-place amongst you, that I may bury my dead out of my sight." The answer portrays to us, as though it were the event of yesterday, the Hittite view of him who wandered up and down their country the friend of God alone. "Thou art a mighty prince amongst us, in the choice of our sepulchres bury thy dead" (Gen. xxiii. 6). With grand oriental solemnity "the mighty prince amongst them" bows himself down before the children of the land, and declines to share with them in death, as he could not share with them in life, and weighs out to them in shekels of silver, current money with the merchants, the full price of Machpelah's cave.

Eight-and-thirty years later the stone was rolled from the cavern's mouth, and Isaac and Ishmael bore another honoured corpse into the shelter of that tomb. Abraham was laid beside Sarah his wife. The long toil, the many ventures, the faithful service, the joyful communing with Jehovah — these were over. The mighty faith which God's love had kindled, which many prayers had fed, which many trials had perfected, had lasted on even to the end, and "Abraham gave up the ghost and died in a good old age, an old man and full of years, and was gathered to his people."

JACOB.

THE life of Isaac succeeds to that of Abraham in the sacred record like the vision of some peaceful lake into which the full waters of a giant river have poured their majestic flow; and which mirrors motionless back the sky above and the mountains round it. Stillness, instead of wandering, was the new condition of his outward life; and the inward answered to it. A calm, meditative, unimpassioned man, conscious of possessing a life given as a marvel, of being the channel of promises which should reach on to the ends of time, his religious character seems to have been summed up in Jacob's words, "The God of my fathers, the God of Abraham, and *the fear of Isaac*" (Gen. xxxi. 42); he dwelt all his days under the safe shadow of the fear of God. All his life, as often happens, was figured forth in that great act of self-sacrifice which marked his early manhood. For such was his willing ascent of the mountain of Moriah at the bidding of Jehovah, and his unresisting submission to being bound for sacrifice on the wood of the burnt-offering which he had meekly borne up the mountain-side. It is the nature of such a life of early devotion to God to be free from the great crises, trials, and agonies by which later conversions and renewals are effected and brought to perfection. It is one long period of unbroken restfulness, leaving, from the very tranquillity with which it was blessed, little to record for others; and tending to develop in the man himself a character of peace rather than of strength. These features we may trace in Isaac. He was a quiet, prosperous, religious man. He sowed and "received an hundred fold, and the Lord blessed him; he waxed great, and went forward, and grew until he became very great, for he had possession of flocks, and possession of herds, and great store of servants, and the

Philistines envied him" (Gen. xxvi. 12—14). In the midst of this envy he was unwarlike and peaceable, trusting in God's protection, and little disposed to self-assertion. Thus, time after time, he yields to the herdsmen of Gerar the wells that he has digged, till they cease to strive for them (Gen. xxvi.). And the same character reappears in his patient acquiescence in the contentions which in later years disturbed his family. This life of calm was for the most part spent in the neighbourhood of that spring of water which the angel of God had shown to Hagar when she was sent forth with Ishmael from the tent of his father. "Isaac dwelt by the well Lahai-roi." There, it seems, when he was himself sixty years old, and twenty years after his marriage, his twin sons, Esau and Jacob, were born.

God's prophetic answer in interpreting the struggling of the unborn children had already foretold to Rebekah the great issue of that birth, in the two nations which should spring from it, of which "the one people should be stronger than the other, and the elder should serve the younger" (Gen. xxv. 23). The different characters of her two sons soon declared themselves. The calm quietness of Isaac's tent was irksome to her firstborn, Esau. He cared not for the pastures which fed his father's many flocks. The wild grounds of the neighbouring desert, with the excitement of the chase of its game, and of conflicts with its beasts of prey, were more congenial to his spirit; and into these he cast himself, mingling in them freely with the children of the land, amongst whom he was soon a leader, as he grew up "a cunning hunter, a man of the field." Closer connection with them naturally followed; and when he was forty years old he took two wives of that Canaanitish blood with which the family of Abraham had never mingled, and "which were a grief of heart and bitterness of spirit unto Isaac and Rebekah." The touches which sketch his character are few, but they are most expressive. We see before us the bold, wild, impetuous, generous, spirited, popular Arab, full of impulse, unsuspicious, uncontrolled, ready to purchase immediate gratification at any price; unable to appreciate the distinctive spiritual blessings which belonged to him as the heir of the great father of the faithful. In him, even more plainly than in Ishmael himself, the Arab son of Abraham, the distinctive unworldly character of the separated friend of God seemed to have lapsed back into the mere son of the world. And so it is a rise in his position when by another sudden act of his impulsive nature, on Jacob being sent to take a wife of the old stock of the Abrahamic family, he, as though to retrieve the character of his married life, takes a third wife of the family of Ishmael, the son of the bond-servant. This essential worldliness of character was connected, as it so often is, especially in youth, with many attractive qualities. Wherever we meet him there is about him a generous recklessness which, though really compatible of union with the highest reign of thoughtless selfishness, yet wears to one who does not look below the surface an aspect of unselfishness which at once wins for him a great amount of sympathy.

Jacob's character was in almost every respect the opposite of Esau's; and in youth at least far less naturally attractive. He was "a plain man, dwelling in tents." Whichever of its disputed meanings we attach to the epithet "plain," it does not greatly alter the aspect of Jacob's character; perhaps the highest is the nearest to the truth; he was a cultivated as his brother was a rough man; a man of the tent, as the other was a man of the forest, the hill-side, and the waste. His taste was for the flocks and herds, for domestic cares and pursuits. As the natural result of the common instincts of our nature, he was the mother's, as Esau was the father's favourite. The somewhat inactive character of Isaac delighted in the daring of his hunter son, whilst the mother found in her more civilised child a companionship and sympathy which she could never taste in the company of the wild man of the desert, the husband of Hittite wives whom she abhorred. Though, moreover, in Jacob's early life there is no more mark of godliness than there is about that of Esau, yet there must in the younger son have been always present that substratum of affectionateness of heart which is the special character of his after years, and which is always so dear to a mother's soul. Jacob's natural character combined remarkably the distinctive features of both his parents. It repeated much of his father's musing, meditative temperament, whilst the stronger passions of his mother's nature stirred its depths to bursts of feeling unknown to Isaac, and whilst there was joined with it the shrewd business powers which seem to have pervaded the family of Laban. His unenterprising home life was in him probably in part the consequence and in part the cause of a certain timidity of nature; which must have shrunk from very close contact with his rough and daring brother. The visits of Esau to the tent beside the waters of Lahai-roi could have been no time of enjoyment for Jacob. Doubtless they drew closer together the bonds between himself and Rebekah, whilst he felt himself eclipsed in the view of the old patriarch, who ate gladly of his favourite son's venison, and listened with wondering admiration to the stories of the adventures and the risks through which Esau's quiver and his bow had secured the welcome game.

Thus the mother's influence would be great with Jacob, and it would almost surely tend to evil. Such a man must be sorely tempted to gain by intrigue what natural force secured for his brother—and the spirit of intrigue is an inherent attribute of the Arab woman. As the desert nourished the fierce independence of Esau's nature, so would Rebekah nurse the lurking subtlety of Jacob's heart. There would be, moreover, a certain aspect of piety about her scheming conduct. Deep in the mother's heart lay the old prophetic utterance, "The elder shall serve the younger;" it was the Will of God that this beloved son, who cowered before his braggart brother, should live to be his lord. She had not learned that deep lesson of faith, the leaving God to work out His Will in His own way. She must help forward its accomplishment. She would possess the mind of Jacob with the same idea. In their after converse, in times of peace and hope, still more, perhaps, when Esau's unwelcome presence drove them into closer and yet more intimate relations, she would fill his heart with visions which belonged to that yet to be accomplished prophecy which Isaac perhaps had never heard, perhaps had long since forgotten. The securing the fulfilment of this prediction by any means would by little and little become with Jacob, as with his mother, the ruling idea with which his mind was full. Its first recorded outbreak was when at thirty-two years of age he tempted his hungry brother to sell his birthright for the savoury mess of lentile pottage. Here the opposite characters of the two men stand out in the boldest relief. The impulsive Bedouin hunter, returning half-famished from some unsuccessful chase, saying under the constraining influence of appetite, "What profit shall this birthright do me?" and so for a momentary enjoyment sacrificing the religious and the temporal rights which by patriarchal use belonged to the first-born; acting herein as a "profane person," as a thorough man of this world, yielding up the future, even the spiritual future, for the immediate and the carnal. Jacob, on the other hand, thoughtful, and given to anticipations of the future; eager to please the mother whom he loved, seeing an opportunity of securing what she had taught him that God meant him to possess, and so with a meanness bred of a subtle intellect, of misleading affections, of a timid temper, and of a debased religiousness, tempted his brother to a sin by which he was himself to profit. Here is the cunning hunter, the man of the field outwitted, as he always is, by the polished man dwelling in the tent.

The next great scene of the two lives, five-and-thirty years later, is when by another act of subtlety he steals away the blessing as he had meanly purchased the birthright of the first-born. Here all the lines are darker. Rebekah is yet more visibly the tempter. Her son, more timid, perhaps less deceitful than herself, shrinks from the perfidy of abusing the darkened sight of his aged father. But she overbears his resistance. She has now persuaded herself that it is well to lie for God, that the great just God of Truth can be helped in the government of His world by a cunning, devil-born falsehood; and she succeeds in her plot, and the younger son secures the blessing.

Here again Esau's character breaks out into most indicative revelations. The wild despair, the passionate pleading, the cry for another blessing—with no apparent sense of the greatness of his higher loss, but with a keen perception of the present evil, and so the cry for a temporal if he could not have the spiritual blessing—here are the evident utterances of a character all impulse; venting its sadness in the unspoken thought that when the old man, whose heart it would grieve, was at rest, he would slay his traitor brother, and so wipe away at once the injury and the insult.

It needed no speaking out of the revengeful purpose to alarm Rebekah. The dark, silent, strong-willed woman used to watch with that keen eastern observance of hers every turn of countenance and tone and manner in her strange wild son of the desert, read it all at a glance. She had gained her point; Jacob had won both the birthright and the blessing, but she had imperilled his life, and she must save it.

There is a deep strain of artifice in her next device. She wakes up in the old father's heart its aching remembrance of Esau's unholy marriages, in order to exalt her younger born.

Rebekah said unto Isaac, "I am weary of my life because of the daughters of Heth: if Jacob take a wife of the daughters of Heth, such as these which are the daughters of the land, what good shall my life do me?" (Gen. xxvii. 46.)

Again she succeeds. Isaac sends away his son from the threatening danger which he knew not of, to find a wife from the daughters of his mother's house. She succeeds, but at what a cost! She loses the son of her love; has to bear henceforward a solitary life; has to live alone; to die alone. For those eyes, it seems clear, see the beloved one again no more for ever. She is not mentioned on his return, and the presence of Deborah, her nurse, with the family of Jacob, as they come back from Padan-aram, goes far to prove the previous death of her mistress. The busy, scheming head was laid low in the dust, it may be weighed prematurely down by the sorrowful harvest she had sown in deceitfulness to reap in anguish.

A new reach of Jacob's life opens with his separation from his mother. The hand of God had taken him into the wilderness there to plead with him mightily. It was a long and a bitter pleading. His own old sin returns before him time after time, as if its haunting presence never would leave him. He had sinned by treachery against his near of kin, and the treachery of those near of kin to him embitter all his life. First, there is Laban's great and often-repeated perfidy. As he had consented to his mother's voice, and lied to his blind father to win the elder brother's portion, so his mother's brother lies to him to win for the elder daughter the marriage he offers to the younger. Into this one master fraud were gathered up for him the seeds of all the long sorrows which darkened his after life. From this came the other great deceit which whitened before the time the hairs of his head; when his own elder sons, hating their younger brother, the child of his beloved Rachel, because his own heart was bound up with the life of the lad, sell Joseph into Egypt; and as he had deceived Isaac with the flesh and the skins of the kid, so they deceived him by dipping in the kid's blood the coat of many colours. Surely God was purging out of the soul of his servant this close-clinging evil even by the hotness of the furnace fire. For coincidently with these retributive sorrows God was giving to him another and a yet deeper teaching. The griefs and injuries of life, if sent alone, might only have hardened and embittered him. But this inner teaching gave to them their special character and power of moral healing.

That inner teaching began at once on Jacob's separation from his mother. Half his life was then spent—spent amidst the enervating and lowering influences of inaction, and want of responsibility, of timidity, flavoured by a certain natural subtlety which was encouraged by the mother, whose influence over him was supreme. With all these elements of weakness abounding in him, he is cast suddenly forth into the wilderness, the perils of which his martial brother loved, but which he had always dreaded. The home-loving, timid, thoughtful man is forced to rely upon and act altogether for himself. On one misty, ill-apprehended belief alone can he at all rest his anxious spirit. There is a future before him. In himself the great promises for which Abraham had wandered and Isaac had waited, now surely centred He had the birthright and the blessing. To that mysterious future his mother's voice, with all her faults, had ever taught him to look forward. Here was the point of difference between himself and Esau. Esau lived for the present, he lived for the future. That dim, uncertain outline ever before his eye gave to life in him a meaning and a depth which it could never have in the clear, bright, dancing, sunlit, but shallow, waters of his brother's objectless being. That worldly spirit lacked utterly the receptive faculty to which higher communications could address themselves. Jacob's soul was ready for them. And they were given to him. As he journeys towards Haran, he lights at eventide upon a certain place. The red sun, like a wearied giant proudly flinging himself to rest, goes down with sudden speed below the wide horizon. The benighted wanderer makes the hasty preparation which alone is possible, and prepares his hard pillow of the desert stones. The bright stars fade away before his weary eyes, and he sleeps. Then the vision wakes. He sees the mystic ladder joining together earth and heaven; he marks with wonder the ascending and descending angels, and he hears the voice of the personal God; with him there in the waste as much as in the tent of Isaac; gathering into shape and form that misty future on which his mind had ever dwelt; and above all, promising to him a perpetual presence and a constant guard. "I am with thee, and will keep thee. I will not leave thee until I have done that which I have spoken to thee of" (Gen. xxviii. 15). He awoke with a sense of God's nearness to him, which made the very place "dreadful." The vision of the night-watches had changed everything around him. There was no loneliness now in that unpeopled waste: it was full of God. Its monotonous stillness was gone. The morning breeze which swept over him, the leaves which rustled under its breath, the brawling waters of the brook, all re-echoed the voice which still rung in his ears. The track of the sunbeams as it lay broad and bright upon the land, spoke to him of the glorious pathway of light which had joined together the heaven and the earth.

Everywhere God was around him. Everywhere God was close beside him. The great training of his spirit had begun. That close, perpetual presence of the personal God made life another thing. It was not for him to weave cunning schemes with sharp, dishonourable subtlety in order to bring to pass the purposes of the great God, who had said to his inmost spirit, "*I* will not leave thee until *I* have done that which I have spoken to thee of." The answer of Jacob's heart is immediate, though it betrays much remaining darkness. There is the "If God will be with me and bring me again, then the Lord shall be my God." The light of God's verity is breaking through, and manifestly scattering the darkness.

With this new light, he goes on his journey, and reaches "the people of the east." Then follows his long service with Laban, and his own practical experience of what deceit is. By it all he is driven to rest himself on that mysterious presence which is now shed around his being; and as he communes with that, he sees the stains upon his own life, the weakness of his own heart.

And so the work within advances. For one-and-twenty weary years he labours and toils at Padan-aram: the drought consumes him by day, and the frost by night, until the hand which others saw not seemed through his reading of Laban's altered countenance to beckon him to depart. He sets out on his return. Some remains of his old self-trusting subtlety, not yet purged out of his heart, lead to his secret flight, and bring on him at once the threatening pursuit of Laban. From this great danger God's direct interference alone delivers him. The recollections of the long past, God's visitation, God's promises, the revelation of his own feebleness and sin—these crowd around him as he retraces his way. He needs them all, for his life is full of peril. He must pass beside the border of the hill country, in which Esau, his injured brother, had grown into a warlike tribe. Now would come, his heart whispered to him, the long-delayed day of reckoning. The more he had learned to see the true character of his own faithless falsehood, the more terrible that danger must have looked. He prepares for it as best he may; but his heart, made tender by discipline, bled for the wife of his love and the children God had given him. But his God had not forgotten His servant. He saw and pitied the weaknesses of His child. At Mahanaim he is met by the angelic host, whose footsteps he had seen upon the heavenly ladder, one-and-twenty years before. But he needs more strength yet, and a greater vision is before him. At the ford Jabbok he sends on before him his wives, his eleven children, and all that he has, and remains himself alone behind—doubtless for unwitnessed, undisturbed communion with his God. It was not in vain that he was led to wait for it. "Jacob," is the mysterious record, "was left alone, and there wrestled a man with him till the breaking of the day," when the unknown stranger said, "Let me go, for the day breaketh." But the mighty one who wrestled with him strengthened him for the unearthly struggle, and the opened and ennobled heart of the long-tried patriarch put forth its last strength in that passionate cry for aid, "I will not let thee go, except thou bless me." The loving discipline of the Almighty had done its work. Close and yet closer his God had drawn to him; and by that near presence, the work of purifying his inmost spirit had been mercifully accomplished. A new name, given him by God, sealed his new character; the meanness of the supplanter was gone; the royal spirit was come. Jacob, "the supplanter," was turned into Israel, "a prince with God." Though the sorrows which chastised his early sin were not yet exhausted; though he had yet to bear the shame of Dinah's fall, the grief of his heart at Simeon's and Levi's cruel and treacherous vengeance; yet from this time a new atmosphere is round about him: he is delivered from Esau; he reaches safely his father's house; he joins with Esau in the solemn burial of Isaac. Again the mysterious cave at Machpelah is opened; again united brothers bear into its shadows the aged form of another father. Isaac is at rest; and Esau and Jacob are at peace; they meet and they part in concord. Each of the brothers had, indeed, received that to which their separate instincts all along had pointed. For the spiritual blessing Esau had never longed. Temporal prosperity and earthly power were the inheritance which he had connected with the birthright and the blessing; and these had come to him, and he was content. Jacob, even in the darkness of his earlier years, had longed for the spiritual gift which still hung in misty outline before him; and all, and more by far than all, to which that desire had pointed had been vouchsafed to him; and for it he was well content to have endured those searching, cleansing years of sorrow, the sharp handling of which he had known. The two brothers part to meet no more, but they part in peace. They share between them their father's goods; the old jealousy and wrath have died out, even of memory: the planter of a new tribe, the head of the future race of the Edomites, takes his " wives, and his sons, and his daughters, and all the souls of his house; and his cattle, and his beasts, and all his substance which he had got in the land of Canaan, and went into the country from the face of his brother Jacob; for their riches were more than that they might dwell together. . . . Thus dwelt Esau in Mount Seir; Esau is Edom."

But the great patriarch's course was not yet accomplished. Few and evil, as he afterwards, on retrospect, esteemed the days of the years of his pilgrimage, he had yet twenty-five of them to spend. Chequered they still were with many sorrows. The punishment of "the supplanter's" subtlety lasted on after its guilt had been forgiven to the Prince with God. He had yet to weep over the jealous hatred which the offspring of Leah and the handmaidens bore to Rachel's beloved son; he had yet, when the cruel deceitfulness of the ten brethren, that fruit of Laban's treachery, had sent him the coat of many colours, stained, as he believed, with Joseph's blood, to mourn sadly forth his sorrow when "he refused to be comforted, and said, For I will go down into the grave to my son mourning;" he had yet to part with Benjamin, and say, "If I am bereaved of my children, I am bereaved."

The especial character of these last years of the patriarch's life is one of deep and lively affectionateness. This is traceable at every turn, and gives its colour to the whole scene. There is an intense humanity about his character which wakes up in every heart a filial feeling of reverential love towards the aged man. We see this in the conduct of the great Pharaoh towards his vizier's father. How grand in its simplicity is the inspired record of this remarkable meeting between the old desert chief and the haughty Pharaoh! The king's question seems to point to the stamp of extreme age as set already on those venerable features—"How many are the days of the years of thy life?" "Few and evil" the old man pronounces them to have been; and then, with the eastern solemnity of age, gives to the Egyptian king the blessing of Jehovah.

How in point of picturesque interest have the two sons of Isaac now changed their places! Esau in his youth is a far more attractive character than Jacob. But who ever dwells on his later years, as we fashion them forth to ourselves in his strongholds on the Mount Seir, the rich, successful, mighty Arab chief, as we rest on those of Jacob? It is the true, ever self-repeating history of the world's banquet; the best wine is that which is first, and afterwards that which is worse. The very lands of the two brothers' inheritance seem to catch up and repeat the mighty truth. The red ranges of the mountains of Edom shine forth gloriously under the blaze of the morning sunshine; but the calm shadows of evening sleep peacefully on the grassy uplands of Judah. There is a difference deep as eternity between natural attractiveness and the true character of redeemed humanity wrought by however slow degrees in the servant of God by the regenerating, renewing influences of the Holy Ghost. It is best, after all, to be indeed on God's side in His world. Brightly as the morning of the man of the world may glow with all the glorious colours of the molten light, it must end in darkness. Showy and attractive as are youthful frankness, joyousness, and daring, there is a poison which pervades and at last destroys all worldly things which are not sanctified by the presence of God; whilst the path of those who walk with God is like the shining light which shineth ever more and more unto the perfect day. And though we are indeed taught as to Esau himself nothing more in his "finding no room for repentance" than that his repentance was too late to bring back to him the blessing of his father's birthright which he had profanely bartered away for the mess of pottage, we are in parable instructed that there may come to every one a time when his probation is over; when for him too it is "too late;" when the bitter cry cannot unlive the life which has been spent in sin; when the heavenly birthright has been lost, and cannot be re-won.

> "Watch by our father Isaac's pastoral door—
>   The birthright sold, the blessing lost and won,
> Tell, Heaven has wrath that can relent no more,
>   The grave dark deeds that cannot be undone.
> We barter life for pottage; sell true bliss
>   For wealth or power, for pleasure or renown;
> Thus, Esau-like, our Father's blessing miss,
>   Then wash with fruitless tears our faded crown."*

As Jacob draws nearer to his end, the halo round his withered brow glows with yet brighter colours. The sorrows of the past are a departing vision; the bitter breaking up of his life from the tent of Isaac, and the companionship of his mother; the cruel treachery of Laban; the loss

* "Christian Year." Second Sunday after Trinity.

of Rachel, the well-beloved wife; the quarrels and the scandals of his family—all, one by one, melt away in the distance. The one remaining and ever-increasing idea of that life is the presence of God with it; the vision before his going down into Egypt gradually expands over and covers the canvas; other voices die away; this only he hears—"I am God, the God of thy father; fear not. I will go down with thee into Egypt" (Gen. xlvi. 3, 4). Seventeen years he spent there in that blessed companionship; seeing Joseph's greatness and the wonderful multiplication of his seed; and then "the time drew nigh that Israel must die." And round his dying bed the powers of the world to come arrayed themselves, and there fell on him the breath of clear, exalted prophecy. From the shadows of his own coming end, his eye ranged on along the ages until, in prophetic foresight, he saw the Conqueror of death. A stranger himself, tarrying for a season in the land of ancient sovereignties, he speaks of his own, as yet subject, race as royal, and of its rule as universal: "The sceptre shall not depart from

Judah, nor a lawgiver from between his feet, until Shiloh come, and unto Him shall the gathering of the people be" (Gen. xlix. 10). What more, after such an utterance, could he do than "gather up his feet into the bed, and yield up the ghost, and be gathered unto his people?" (Gen. xlix. 33.)

JOSEPH.

THE narrative of Joseph's life is the connecting link in the sacred volume between the story of a single life and the history of a people. In his day the covenant life spread itself into wider circles. In Abraham it was summed up in one man; when Isaac was born it flowed on into him. In Jacob it enlarged itself into the family; in the days of Joseph it swelled out into the dimensions of a tribe. Yet though he was mainly instrumental in this development, he was not the head of the tribe, nor was it through his line that the blessing to convey which to all nations Israel was constituted a separate people, came to the family of man. And so it is the history of the man, and not that of the tribal head, which rivets us in the life of Joseph.

He comes before us overshadowed by the great love of his father Jacob. He was the son of Jacob's old age: he was the child of the beloved Rachel. When his history begins Benjamin was too young (but one year old), to bear the great weight of that passionate affection. Still to the old man's feelings Joseph was the son of "Rachel my wife." This love for Rachel threw a golden light over the old patriarch's last years. Deep, enduring, absorbing, unselfish love, especially for those parted from us by the dark veil which separates us from the unseen world, exalts humanity. And this is always showing itself in Jacob. The bitter lamentation for Deborah, and the planting over her grave the terebinth of tears, because she had been Rachel's nurse, and was the last living link left of those maiden days of youth and beauty, is a lively mark of the old man's enduring love: so is the description of her as "My wife, who bare me two sons" (Gen. xliv. 27), as if she alone and her offspring rose up to the true dignity of the family life. So is the pouring out of his heart on that sick bed to which Joseph brought his two sons for their parting blessing. The old man looks upon their young strength, and the past years, fleet as their wont is before his failing eyes, until the one thought, which was never far distant, rises before him, and as though from that sad day his life of lives was spent, he sums up all in the plaintive utterance, "And as for me, when I came from Padan, Rachel died by me in the land of Canaan in the way, when yet there was but a little way to come unto Ephrath: and I buried her there in the way of Ephrath; the same is Bethlehem." It was as if again the old deceit looked in on his soul in those thoughts of sadness. For he had been sent to bring his wife from Padan to Canaan, and he came back with her to the border she was not to pass; came back to enter his father's tent alone, having left Rachel at Bethlehem; and to find Rebekah laid before her at Mamre.

Of all this great love Joseph was the natural inheritor, and in the wild Arab family which had grown up round Jacob he was the only one whose personal qualities in any way fitted him for so rich a possession. The discord, the license, the sensuality, and the cruelty which so disfigured the sons of Jacob, were but a reflection of what might have been seen in all the common life of the world around them in still darker colours. No doubt it was a great falling back towards heathendom when it is compared with the family life of Abraham and of Isaac. This was the inevitable consequence of that great curse of Jacob's life, the marriage with Leah palmed on him through Laban's treachery. The sons of that ill-matched union, of the rival sisters and their rival handmaids, had lost from before their eyes that true aspect of the life of the family which had shown so fair in Isaac's tent. To Joseph only was it shown in that strong transferred affection which almost made his dead mother stand as though still alive before him. To him that old man was ever in his tender love as well mother as father. This of itself tended not a little to elevate and purify the young heart of the motherless son. Beyond this, the father's love evidently succeeded in stamping upon the boy the impress of his own spiritual life. The distinguishing feature of

Jacob's religious character was his enduring sense of God's perpetual presence with him. The lesson of the heavenly ladder dwelt ever in his heart. This stole early into Joseph's inmost spirit with the accesses of his father's love, and we shall find it reappearing at each crisis of his life as the father's grace repeated in the son.

When at seventeen years old he is suffered to leave that father's side, and begin his own life-work of tending the flocks on the low plains or wild uplands of Canaan, it is with the sons of Zilpah and of Bilhah that he is sent, as being the nearest to himself in age. But his moral sense is already above theirs; God's presence makes their youthful sins intolerable to him, and he brings unto his father the report of their evil doings. Such a course was of itself sufficient to stir up against him the angry passions of such brothers as were at this time the sons of Jacob. Their father's conduct increased the evil. His fondness for Joseph broke out into irritating manifestations of partiality. Whilst they were habited in the ordinary dress of Arab shepherds, for the favourite son was provided the long-sleeved tunic, which in that eastern land belonged to superior rank; and all Jacob's conduct manifested the same peculiar and distinguishing affection.

These angry feelings were exasperated by Joseph repeating to them two dreams which he had dreamed. In the first of these, as they bound sheaves together in the field their sheaves gathered round and did obeisance unto his; in the second the sun and the moon and the eleven stars made obeisance to him. The first of these seemed to foretell that he should be the chiefest of all the family, and that all his brethren should bow down to him. This moved their indignation greatly; and their wrath knew no bounds when this dream was followed by the second, both because, according to the notions of those days, its repetition of the leading idea marked the fulfilment of the first as certain, and also because it added the new prediction that his father and his mother would unite with his brethren in doing homage to him. Even the loving heart of Jacob was stirred by this, and he reproved with some sharpness what seemed to him the ambitious imaginations of his favourite son. The father's words seem to imply that he felt it as some indignity to that memory of the dead mother which as a sacred lamp within a sepulchre burned evermore in his widowed heart; and though he could not but "observe the saying," yet he rebuked the dreamer. The brethren saw in it the fulfilment of all the fears which their father's over-partiality, and especially the gift of the vest of honour, had aroused in them. They knew, doubtless, the story of the birthright stolen through Rebekah's craft from the first-born of the last generation: and that craft was still being punished in the hard thoughts which now rose in their minds against both their father and their brother. He who had consented to violate the rights of his own elder brother might easily, they thought, be led to break through the same rights again in another generation to gratify his partial fondness for the son of his old age. So with a new and an embittered aversion "they hated Joseph yet the more for his dreams and for his words."

But what shall we say of the dreams themselves, and of Joseph's conduct with regard to them? Are we to take them as direct revelations, as one of those visions from God which have, we know, ere now fallen in sleep upon his servants, and ordered and guided their way? It is not said so in Holy Writ, and there is no such declaration as that God appeared unto Joseph in a dream. We are left, therefore, to gather from the context what their character was; and we cannot settle this without having some idea concerning all dreams; and not concerning dreams only, but concerning those waking visions which visit our own minds and the minds of others; which seem bred of no suggestion from the immediate present, but arise in them spectre-like and unbidden,—the clear air fashioning itself into strange forms, and the heart's silence breaking into words which to the inner consciousness seem almost articulate.

Whence come these, and what are they? Are they the mere reachings forth of our own spirit; prophecies of the future because they are the utterances of our own present capacities and deepest longings; unborn acts stirring in the womb of the imagination, and waiting their time of birth? Or are they often more than this? Are they purposes and desires of good or of evil which have been wakened up by the sweeping over the waters of our soul of the breath of the unseen enemy, or of the gusts bred of past passions; or, on the other hand, by the sweet, healing, and enlightening presence of that blessed Spirit which bloweth where it listeth? Who can read the secret of these hidden influences? Who can separate the voice of his own inner being, as original creation framed it, and as past life has moulded it, from the stirring of its sleeping chords, by the sweep over them of these invisible airs?

Here, then, we may come to some clearer idea of the true character of the dreams of Joseph. All those mighty gifts of government which his after life developed, were even now lying seed-like and half fashioned within his soul. Over that soul swept the Spirit of his father's God, ripening for perfection, and half awakening these dormant faculties; and as they were thus stirred, the busy, creative imagination caught their shapes and consequences, and cast them in their coming colours upon the receptive half-consciousness of the soul in sleep. To this half-natural fore-reaching of his spirit, the higher Spirit, we may well believe, added for him, whose after life would so greatly need such supports, a clearness of perception not its own, and which, if it was not directly prophetic, savoured of prophecy.

Whilst, then, we must not class the dreams of Joseph with those visions of Daniel, in which the strong and direct breath of the Divine Spirit swept before his sleeping eyes the course of dynasties and empires and ages; nor separate them altogether from the inborn prophecies wherewith great minds forecast their own future; neither can we altogether deny to them the character of being inspirations from the Spirit of God. Only, in so accounting of them, let us duly realise the truth that such a view ought not, in our estimate, so much to divorce the supernatural from Joseph's life as to wed it to our own; that it ought to enable us better to comprehend the unity which exists between the patriarchal dispensation and the Christian; to see how that which afterwards for a stiff-necked generation was fixed and almost congealed into the Urim and the Thummim, floated for those earlier saints, and floats for us, an ever-present, impalpable, but most real Power, round about our bed and our path, acting according to its own spiritual laws upon our own inmost and essential spirits. Have we not ourselves known young hearts which seem so to have been visited? The youth of after greatness not rarely has upon it some mark of such a presence. The lad is incomprehensible to his fellows. The frivolous, the sensual, the hollow, the sons of Bilhah and Zilpah, feel his very presence to be the sending up of their evil report to the Great Father. They would that he were like themselves. "Mad" they call him in our schools and colleges; for he lives apart from full companionship with others. If every now and then he joins with a spasmodic earnestness in their games and recreations, for the most part he keeps aloof from them; is full of speculation; wanders objectless over the playground, wondering within himself at the life that is stirring in his breast,—wondering whether it so stirs in others; trying to track its laws; dreaming of its development, until the sun, the moon, and the eleven stars, seem to do obeisance to him in some unknown future which spreads out mist-like before him.

Such then, we may apprehend the dreams of Joseph to have been. His ready divulgence of them agrees exactly with this view. His own soul was full of them; he craved for sympathy. They prefigured he knew not exactly what. He hardly realised in the vista they opened to his eyes, that his elevation was, to a certain extent, the subjection of the rest; and so, with none of the pettiness of vanity, and very little of the chastening of prudence, he told them openly, and thus aggravated his brethren's hatred, and drew upon himself what was harder yet to bear —the blighting frost of his father's displeasure, nipping the tender buds of his yet half-formed anticipations.

Neither he nor his father could fathom the depths of his brothers' hatred. In no portion of his life had Jacob been tempted to it, and the loving spirit of his old age knew nothing of such darkness. And so, when the brethren had been some time away feeding their flocks upon the as yet unappropriated plains and uplands, the father fearlessly sends his darling to inquire after their welfare; and Joseph, unconscious of the deep grudge he had engendered, undertakes with ready dutifulness the distant mission. He goes first from Hebron to Shechem, seeking them. They were not there. He learns from a wayfarer, as he wanders about searching for them, the direction of their track, and follows them on, some twelve miles north of Samaria, nigh to Dothan. He comes upon them with all the freedom and affection of a brother's heart. But it is only to waken up, by his very aspect, from malicious lips, the evil greeting, "Behold, this dreamer cometh." Then when they saw him afar off, even before he came near unto them, awoke the sinful consultation: "They conspired against him to slay him." There were, indeed, as is the wont of such companies, various degrees of wickedness amongst its members. There were there men in whose tents the "instruments of cruelty" were ready. There were also the sensual softness of Reuben and Judah's uncertainty of purpose, as well as the ruder violence of more hardened offenders, who would at once "slay him and cast him into some pit, and say some evil beast hath devoured him, and we shall see what will become of his dreams" (Gen. xxxvii. 20). Reuben's counsel to "shed no blood" succeeds, and so they seize him, tear from him the hated vest of honour, cast him into a dry pit, and sit down to eat bread. As they make their meal, the huge forms of the "ships of the desert," the camels of the merchants' caravan, rise on their sight. A caravan of Ishmaelites is journeying from Gilead through the plain of Dothan to join the great track which passed from Canaan by Gaza into Egypt. At once the uncertain mind of Judah, trembling with horror at the thought of the great sin of leaving Joseph to perish in the pit, and yet not brave enough to propose his absolute release, seizes on the thought of a safe compromise, and proposes to sell him to the merchants of Midian. In the absence of Reuben, who had intended privily to release the lad, the sale is effected. The merchants pay for him the usual price, and carry him away. When Reuben, on his return, finds the pit empty and his scheme frustrated, he rent his clothes and cried, "The child is not, and I, whither shall I go?" Whether from the struggling of a natural pity, or from fear of bringing down with utter grief to the grave the grey-haired man at home, whose life he knew was bound up with the lad's life, he alone enters into all the horror of the tragedy. He does not over-rate the agony which was about to tear that loving heart.

They dip the vest of honour, with which it had been the old man's delight to clothe Joseph, in the blood of a kid, and with a triumph, which they cannot but give vent to in their very words, they send it to him with the lying message, "This have we found: know now whether it be thy son's coat or no." Too well the father knew it: too surely did it seem to him that he inherited afresh the sins of his youth, as he cried, "An evil beast hath devoured him! Joseph, no doubt, is rent in pieces." Many days he mourned, refusing to be comforted; and groaning forth, "I will go down mourning into Sheol, that dark land of shadows, where my son has passed before me."

Whilst Hebron echoes these groans of a broken heart, Joseph is carried down into Egypt, and finds a ready purchaser in Potiphar, the captain of the executioners of Pharaoh's house. His master's name, when read in the light which the study of hieroglyphics throws upon it, seems to make it clear that the town of On, devoted to the worship of "Ra," the sun, was the spot of Joseph's servitude. Here he wins at once, because "the Lord is with him," the favour and trust of his master, and is employed in an universal oversight of his concerns. The sculptures of old Egypt depict his life: there we may see the trusted servant overlooking all, entering with minute care, as a patient scribe, every part of his master's property in its daily administration; recording the grain, the fish, the linen, the mass of precious metal, which pass through his hands. Under Joseph's administration all things prospered. It was not only that his great gifts of government were used in his master's service. Beyond this, a higher power was prospering all he touched. "From the time that Potiphar made him overseer in his house and over all that he had, the Lord blessed the Egyptian's house for Joseph's sake; and the blessing of the Lord was upon all that he had in the house and in the field" (Gen. xxxix. 5). But this life of busy, honest, successful labour was not to last. His master's wife, too true to the type of old Egyptian womanhood, as every ancient chronicle depicts it, first tempts him to sin, and then, infuriated at his holy resistance to her evil will, slakes her uttermost vengeance by throwing, through a false accusation, not, as it seems, entirely believed, nor wholly disbelieved, the too faithful slave into the dungeon where the king's prisoners were bound.

How grand a display all this is of the power of a living inward sense of God's perpetual presence in ennobling the soul of man! For what condition could be more open to temptation than that of this Hebrew lad? How natural would it have been for him, when smarting under the keen sense of his brethren's perfidious cruelty, and its seeming success, to have cast away all belief in right and truth, and so to have sunk down into the despairing slough of utter godlessness and sensuality! What temptations, too, to such a course must have gathered themselves up against him in the absolute loneliness of his first Egyptian life! Home associations, the voice of love, the watching eye of tender care, the acting up to an already established character—what helps are these! and these seemed to be gone from him altogether. How noble to be the same without them, to have no lowering of the standard from the loss of all outward safeguards, no sapping of the foundations of moral responsibility from his loss, as a stranger, a foreigner, and a slave, of the elevating sense of personality, and the preserving love of character! How grand still to have, like some lustrous diamond gleaming inwardly on his lonely spirit, the talisman of the one thought—" How can I do this great wickedness and sin against God!" This thought was strong enough so to quicken his conscience, that it still connected indissolubly this broken disconnected present with that old past of his younger life, and whilst he moved amidst the new temptations of the house of the Egyptian, he still lived in thought, and love, and faith, in the old tent at Hebron, and saw the fond face of his aged father, and bowed with him anew before the God of Israel.

This was a safeguard which outward change could not touch; and in the king's dungeon, therefore, Joseph still was what he had been in the house of the captain of the executioners. Great, indeed, at first was the trial of his faith. That he escaped with his life from such an accusation implies, probably, that some doubt of his guilt crossed his master's mind. But it was hard, to bear without discontent and murmur, the dungeon and its cruelty, to have "his feet hurt with fetters, and to be laid in iron" (Ps. cv. 18), as the reward of faithfulness, chastity, and truth. In such a time the evil one was sure to whisper, "Where is thy father's God, and His remembrance of thee? Curse thy God and die." But the darker the natural gloom, the brighter shone that ever-present inward memory of the

God whom he had served at Hebron. He wore the talisman on his heart, and he was safe. Moreover, besides this talisman within the shrine of his own spirit, there was with him an external guardianship which nothing could break through. How magnificent is the simplicity of its announcement!—"Joseph was there in the prison. But the Lord was with Joseph, and showed him mercy, and gave him favour in the sight of the keeper of the prison. . . . . And whatsoever they did there, he was the doer of it . . . . because the Lord was with him, and that which he did the Lord made it to prosper" (Gen. xxxix. 31—33). How long he remained in the prison it is impossible to say with certainty. There and in the house of Potiphar together he spent thirteen years, probably the larger share of them in the prison. Thirteen years of training and perfecting; thirteen years in which the weeds of vanity and self-exaltation were being killed; in which faith and hope and tenderness for other sufferers were matured; in which went on the slow ripening of that genius and those gifts of conduct which were soon to be shown forth upon so high a stage of earthly greatness.

And now, when "the word of the Lord" had indeed "tried him" (Ps. cv. 19), his time came. Two chief officers in Pharaoh's household are put in ward in the prison where Joseph was bound; and Joseph is set by the captain of the ward specially to attend on these great men. How long the attendance had lasted we know not, but it was long enough to form those kindly relations which ever grew up between Joseph and those round him. Accordingly, as he waits upon them he notices one morning their saddened countenances, and with kindly youthful sympathy he asks as to their grief. They answer that they have each dreamed a dream, and they are troubled because there in the dungeon they can consult no interpreter to tell them the meaning of the visions. The Hebrew captive's answer soars at once into a higher sphere—"Do not interpretations belong to God?" "May not He" (he suggests), "the mighty Elohim, send you an answer even by my lips? Tell me the dreams."

The chief of the cup-bearers tells his dream of restoration to royal favour, the master of the household his dream of coming doom; and both are fulfilled within three days, on the birthday of the Pharaoh. Joseph's entreaty to the chief officer of the cup-bearers, and the promise it had won of his making mention to Pharaoh of the unrighteous keeping of the Hebrew youth in the dungeon, are both forgotten in the ecstatic joy of the cup-bearer on his restoration to liberty and power, and so two full years pass on with their weary length, and Joseph, now thirty years of age, and still in prison, has spent thirteen since he was stolen away out of the land of the Hebrews. But now the days of these sorrows were numbered. Pharaoh's two dreams, and his sore trouble at finding no interpreter, bring back to the remembrance of the chief of the cup-bearers the Hebrew slave of the captain of the executioners, and his true reading of the two dreams which had been told him in the prison. From him Pharaoh hears of Joseph, and snatching eagerly at the hope so strangely offered him of obtaining an interpreter, he sends for Joseph from the ward. With such hasty preparation as was possible, the young Hebrew stands before the dreaded throne of Egypt, whether, as seems not impossible, the great Sesostris, or before a monarch of another of the ancient dynasties of Egypt, it mattered little then to him. His life was in his hand; nor easier or more lightly might a man cast a cup of water on the ground, than might that life be thrown away by one frown of the despotic king. Yet unawed and untrembling the youth stands up before the king, because the hidden strength was his. "I have heard say of thee," begins the eager monarch, "that thou canst understand a dream to interpret it." "It is not in me," answers Joseph; "God shall give Pharaoh an answer of peace. God," he boldly declared, "God hath showed Pharaoh what He is about to do," and he reads plainly out to him the riddle of the night's visions. The seven coming years of plenty and the seven following years of famine are declared, and the policy of Pharaoh is marked out for him with an unfaltering tongue.

Again the question rises, which Joseph's own

dreams suggested, whence was this insight he possessed into these four visions, and to what did it amount? Again it must be said that it is nowhere written of Joseph as it is of Daniel, "God made Daniel to understand all visions and dreams" (Dan. i. 17); and though Joseph with a natural piety attributes all his power to the "Elohim," and though Pharaoh so receives it, and justifies to his courtiers the promotion of Joseph to the highest place by the fact that the Spirit of God is in him; yet neither do Joseph's words, nor does the effect on Pharaoh indicate that direct revelation of Jehovah's power, which in the case of Daniel bowed down the proud heart of Nebuchadnezzar to the wonderful acknowledgment, "Your God is a God of gods and the Lord of lords." Narrow indeed, perhaps almost imperceptible, are the barriers which divide the direct illumination vouchsafed by the Revealer of secrets to Daniel from the more ordinary enlightenment given to the holy, thoughtful son of Jacob; and it is well to note how the one passes into the other; as bringing common life more nearly into that august presence with which the heavens are bright, and so adding to it a sacredness and wonder which some would look upon as withheld from ordinary men, and fenced off within the mystic bounds of immediate inspiration.

Looking thus at the record of Genesis, may we not see that God who gave all to Joseph gave him, by means which we call natural, however unusually quickened, the intuition to read what would have been illegible to a shallower or less observant or less enlightened mind? His natural gifts had enabled him to gather first from his communion with the state prisoners whom he tended the probable restoration of the one, the probable execution of the other; to know that the birthday festival would almost necessarily bring to its final issue the fortune of each of these great court officials, and so, when the dream of each presented to his eye in airy imagery the shadow of the coming crisis, the heavenly light fell upon its folds, and he was enabled to read it out with an unfaltering clearness. Pharaoh's dreams themselves, though they rise higher out of the region of simple naturalness in their conception, possessed the same natural tendency to self-explanation when scanned by one who evermore associated his thought of God with the events and destinies of national life, who had learned to understand the great truth that the God of Abraham was the Lord of all, ruling as much over the court of Egypt as in the tent of Hebron. Every field would set before him the thin ears or the fruitful: every reedy pasture by the river bank, that natural image of the whole power of Egypt, the lean kine or the fat, and the cherished secret of God's holy sovereignty might link for him the coming event with the prefiguring image. As the counsel founded on the interpretation, so the interpretation itself, was full of natural insight, though quickened doubtless by the powers of a higher light. Joseph's life was full of God, and so the light of God poured into it; the sinner's life is the shutting out of God, and so his understanding becomes darkened.

With this special gift of insight the long trial of the faithful man passed away, and now dawned the day for which he had so long been trained. The Hebrew slave, yesterday a prisoner in the dungeon, by a change of fortune familiar to Orientals, is to-day Grand Vizier of Egypt, and next only to Pharaoh, its supreme autocrat. In true Eastern fashion, Pharaoh took off his ring (the mystic signet) from his hand, and put it upon Joseph's hand, and arrayed him in vestures of fine linen, and put a gold chain about his neck, and they cried before him, "Bow the knee." Further, he united him, by a marriage with the daughter of the prince-priest of On, to the aristocracy of Egypt. In the name which Joseph gave to her, and in the names of the two sons she bore to him, Joseph testified his resolution, even in that far land, to bind up his family life with the race of Abraham, whilst they speak of his grateful sense of God's care of him in teaching him to forget his sorrows, and in making him fruitful in the land of his captivity.

And now all his gifts of government are drawn forth into action. He goes during the years of plenty through the land, and stores up with careful industry the fruits of the earth whilst it brought forth by handfuls. Then came the years of dearth. Egypt has always been liable to famine. A time of drought at once produced it; and as she was the storehouse of the neighbouring peoples when the same cause exhausted their supplies, they turned to her for help. So it was now. And Joseph, with a wise liberality, opened his stores for them, as well as for Egypt. He would enrich with foreign trade the land which had adopted him, whilst at home he used the opportunity to change and equalise—retaining only the exemptions of the priestly class—the taxation of Egypt.

But wider consequences were to follow from these years of famine. By Him who in His mysterious sovereignty brings His counsels to pass through the natural acting of secondary causes, they were meant to bring down Jacob and his family to Egypt, and so prevent that mixture of the chosen family with the Canaanitish blood, which would have been inevitable if for these early centuries they had remained within the land of promise. Already Judah had mingled the holy seed with the evil race; and had they not been walled in within the land of Goshen, the separation of the race from whom Messiah was to spring would have been impossible. Fulfilling therefore, without knowing it, the counsels of the Highest, the sons of Jacob came down to purchase corn in Egypt. They present themselves before their brother, but they know him not. More than twenty years had stamped their deep impress of sorrow and of joy on the face once in its youthful beauty so familiar to them. In dress, in language, and in manners he was now an Egyptian. The dreams of his youth in the land of Canaan are fulfilled as they bow before him. He witnesses the late awaking of their long-slumbering consciences, he hears their mutual upbraidings; yet still, even to himself, the old imposture is repeated. They tell him, with ambiguous utterance, that "one is not," and yet more plainly still "his brother is dead." The long pent-up affections of his soul are ever ready to break forth as he probes that he may heal their hearts. At length the victory is won. Benjamin is with them, and is guarded by them with all the jealous tenderness of a father's care. Then at last he makes himself known to them, and sends for the old man from Canaan, that he may himself be the stay of those last years, which, after their long sadness, blossomed out again now that the company of Rachel's son seemed to bring her presence back.

What that summons was to Jacob no words can tell save those which broke forth from that long-suffering heart: "It is enough; Joseph my son is yet alive; I will go and see him before I die" (Gen. xlv. 28). Then followed the cheering vision at Beer-sheba, the "Fear not to go down into Egypt. . . . I will go down with thee; and I will also surely bring thee up again; and Joseph shall put his hand upon thine eyes." Safe in that companionship, the old man travelled down to Egypt, and when he came to Goshen the chariot of the Grand Vizier met the cavalcade. If there had been in Joseph's early aspirations something too much of a sense of personal greatness, it was gone now; there was no boast on his side, no rebuking on his father's. "He presented himself unto him; and he fell on his neck, and wept on his neck a good while. And Israel said unto Joseph, Now let me die, since I have seen thy face, because thou art yet alive" (Gen. xlvi. 29, 30). Seventeen years longer that life lasted, and Joseph's figure is seen yet again amidst its last shadows upholding and blessed by the departing patriarch. Then he leads the great company, the chariots and horsemen, the servants of Pharaoh, and the elders of the land of Egypt, who go up with him and with his brethren to bury his father, according to his oath, in the cave of the field of Machpelah, "which Abraham bought with the field, for a possession of a burying-place, of Ephron the Hittite before Mamre."

One more most significant outcoming of the spirit of Joseph yet remains. When the family of Israel had returned to Egypt, to live under the shadow of Joseph, his brethren, whose narrow hearts could not measure the greatness of his love, feared for themselves that the day of long-delayed vengeance might at last be come.

"Joseph will hate us," groaned their evil misgiving hearts, "and will certainly requite us all the evil which we did unto him." So they feigned a dying message of their departed father, praying Joseph to forgive them. The distrust grieved him to the heart, and he wept when they spake unto him. Had he not of old bid them "not to be angry with themselves that they had sold him hither, for God did send me to preserve life;" and had he ceased to see in all that had happened to him the hand of God? "Fear not," he said, with a sobbing voice, "fear not: for am I in the place of God? . . . . . Ye thought evil against me; but God meant it unto good. . . . Fear not: I will nourish you, and your little ones. And he comforted them, and spake kindly unto them" (Gen. l. 21).

With such deeds of love his history ends. And so he too passes out of sight, living until he was an hundred and ten years old, seeing Ephraim's children of the third generation, and taking an oath of the children of Israel, "God will surely visit you, and ye shall carry my bones from hence." So he died strong in the hope of

Israel; bound to it by the ever-during bond of faith; to rise with it at the trumpet's sound from the field of Mamre, though, after the manner of the heathen, "they embalmed him, and he was put in a coffin in Egypt" (Gen. l. 26). His death was like his life—hidden with God; Egyptian in appearance, Hebrew indeed; accomplished in the town of On, amidst pagan dedications to the sun, but tending to the burying-place of Abraham and the resurrection of the heir of all things. Such was Joseph: the link between the wandering patriarch and the lawgiver of nations; touching on the one side the Bedouin fathers of his race, and on the other the kings and mighty princes of the house of Ephraim. He was one who was, like all great men, far in advance of his age; as a ruler of men; as a financier; as combining together an unswerving loyalty to Jehovah with a righteous forbearance towards the debased forms of worship which he found and could not alter in the land which had adopted him; in being capable of being at once an Egyptian patriot and a Hebrew hero. In all these relations he was long before his age. The old patriarchal character broadens out into the politician and the governor of man. Of no other character preserved in all the ancient sacred record is so much told and nothing to his blame. As we dwell upon his life, it is a Christian character which opens on us. Its breadth, its purity, its justice, its forgiveness of injury, its recognising Abraham's God as the father of all —this from first to last is eminently Christian, whilst all is based upon the ever-present sense of God's nearness to him. The motto of the whole life may be found in his simple description of himself—"For I fear God!"

Once more: his life and his character are enchased with the deep lines of typical prophecy. As the true brother condemned and cast out by his own, and saving them through the sacrifice of himself; and then as lifted up from the dungeon to the throne; the son of Israel prophesied in act and in character of the great Hope of Israel. As the captive, oppressed, persecuted, and cast into the dungeon, as revealing in it the will of God, as subduing from it the hearts of men, as inheriting the riches, the learning, and the power of the Egyptians, as ruling by the indwelling Spirit of the Lord, where he had served in the prison as a slave, there are marked upon this history the chiefest lineaments of the Church of Christ, rising from her uttermost persecutions, interpreting the will of God, inheriting the riches of the Gentiles, lifted up from the dunghill to be set amongst the princes, yea, amongst the highest princes of the people. Joseph in the pit and in the prison is the Church in the wilderness; Joseph reigning over Egypt the Church triumphant. For known unto God are all his ways from the beginning of the world.

MOSES.

"IT shall come to pass that at evening time it shall be light" (Zech. xiv. 7). The working of God in Time is evermore, from generation to generation, the fulfilment of this promise. It is when the hour is darkest, when sorrow is heaviest, when hope is dying, when the clouds are thickest, and the hollow moaning of the voice of despair is beginning to awake upon the dull night breeze—it is then that He interferes to whom Time is not, save as the setting wherein He has been pleased to place His work.

So it was, eminently, when Moses was born to be the deliverer of the children of Israel. The darkness of the clouds which veiled their sky hardly could gather into a deeper blackness.

They had long lost the peaceful security of the land of Goshen. There they had multiplied with the unusual increase God had promised to their great forefathers, until they became a terror to the jealous people among whom they tarried. The fame of the great Vizier of their race, before whom Egypt had bowed, had passed away. The internal troubles of the land, the changes of dynasties, and the vicissitudes of events had almost swept away his memory, and long ago another king had arisen who knew not Joseph. What if these Syrian herdsmen were to join with some Arab tribe and subjugate the whole land? This was the ruling terror, and it must be guarded against with all the subtlety of Egyptian policy. One of these guards was found in depressing them to the rank of slaves; in breaking up their sense of independence and nationality, and thus bowing the neck betimes. Another resource was to reduce their numbers by the slaughter of their male children. Both were practised. To the eye of sense the old promise seemed dying out. The fertility of which it spoke had brought their doom upon them, whilst a slavish heart was rapidly being bred within their bosoms. The leeks and the cucumbers, the flesh-pots and the abundance of their store—for these they were growing to long; and their softened, debased spirits bowed to the oppressor's rod, and did, with an abject obedience which their rugged ancestors would have spurned, the foreign tyrant's bidding.

There is no harder task for any man than to rouse up again into life such an expiring national spirit. Woe to him who attempts it, and wavers or fails in his endeavour—the oppressor's utter hatred, and a timid and treacherous abandonment by those whom he has stirred only to bring on them a heavier servitude, is his inevitable end.

This was to be the work of the son of Amram; for this he was born of the family of Levi; for this God's electing purpose had from eternity designated him; for this, in time, God's providence wrought in secret ways to fit, furnish, and perfect His servant. He to whom all things are open, saw that the time was come in which His promise to Abraham should begin to stir towards its fulfilment. He knew that the character of the reigning Pharaoh was that which, by the mingling of obstinacy and fear, was tempered to be the passive instrument of His high designs, and so provided in Moses the fit agent of His will. As under Joseph the family had grown into a tribe, so under Moses the tribe was to be raised into a republic. The formation of such a character as was needful for the fulfilment of the leader's after-work required a long and most varied fashioning—we may read it in the lines of the prophet's life.

Saved from the destruction of the male children of his tribe by an incident familiar to Egyptian life, and a caprice characteristic of an Eastern woman, Moses is brought up as the son of Pharaoh's daughter. For forty years this was his life. In the simple record of his own narrative it is compressed into fifteen verses of the second chapter of Exodus. In the great argument of St. Stephen (Acts vii. 20—29) his brief history swells out into striking facts as to which his humility kept him silent. Thus we read, besides the simple and exquisitely pathetic record of Exodus, speaking across the chasm of three thousand years in whispered words to which every mother's heart still responds, "She saw the child, and the babe wept, and she had compassion on him," that he was "exceeding fair;" thus we read, too, that "he was learned in all the wisdom of the Egyptians, and was mighty in words and deeds."

If we turn from this brief narrative of Holy Writ to what Jewish, Moslem, Heathen, and even Christian legends have recorded of these forty years, the story, keeping the same general outline of fact, expands again marvellously on every side; tradition, according to its wont, playing halo-like in many-coloured hues around the single point of truth. Thus we are told that on the night of his birth all the idols in Egypt were cast down (Weil, "Bible, Koran, and Talmud," p. 96), and that this portent roused the Egyptian priests to seek to destroy the new-born deliverer, of whose advent and mighty deeds they had been already warned by prophetic intimation. "One of the slaves of the daughters of Israel," so ran the warning, "will bear a son, who shall hurl thee and thy people unto the lowest abyss" (Weil, 92). Thus again, to the Scripture record of the beauty of his infant countenance, described both in the Acts and in the Epistle to the Hebrews by a word applied to none beside himself in the New Testament, Josephus adds that it was such that those who met him on the road were forced to turn again, leaving their business behind them, that they might gaze upon him, whilst yet beyond this is added the account that the Pharaoh's daughter who looked at him in the ark was cured at once of the plague of leprosy from which she had long suffered, and the single cure is expanded into that of three of the king's daughters. Then when he is rescued, he refuses the milk of the Egyptian nurse his foster-mother had provided. For "shall the lips which are to speak with the Shekinah touch that which is unclean?" (Weil, 101.)

Who, in Egyptian history, the Pharaoh's daughter was it is not easy to decide, though an ingenious threading together of hieroglyphs and history leads Mr. Osburn to believe that she may be identified with Thouris, daughter of Sesostris, King of Upper Egypt, married by her father, from ambitious motives, to Siphtha, the infant king of Lower Egypt, in whose name she administered the kingdom. Her going down to the sacred river was to fulfil certain sacred rites which her position required at her hands; her ready adoption of the beautiful Hebrew infant a natural result of the childlessness of her enforced wedlock. Thus the " being called the son of Pharaoh's daughter " involved for Moses more than a mere introduction into the royal palace of old Egypt. It was the design of the foster-mother to breed him up as her successor in her royal dignity

Wilder legends yet paint the Egyptian life and exploits of the future lawgiver. His youth, spent in the midst of dangers from the caprice and jealousy of Pharaoh, grows up into a manhood of early power, and even glory. Not only is he learned in all the lore of the then centre of the whole world's civilisation, but he becomes at Heliopolis, Oarsiph, the priest of On, and leads successful armies into Ethiopia.

This reach of his life terminates, in sacred history and legendary lore, at about the age of forty years, and with events generally alike, at least in outline.

He was great, learned, and powerful. There lay before him a future of unlimited earthly splendour. He had the burning aspirations which belong to genius. What would be his course? All the purposes of God for the family of Abraham, all the mighty promises for man which hung on that election, seemed to tremble on the issue of his choice. If he yielded to the temptations of a worldly ambition and chose the throne of the Pharaohs, Israel would become, as other tribes already had become, incorporated with Egypt, the separation of the family of God lost, and the evil world triumphant. But so it was not to be. Already, as a typical fulfilment of a yet greater calling, it was to be accomplished in Moses, "Out of Egypt have I called my son." The Spirit of God brooded on the heaving waters of his yet unenlightened heart. His natural ambition took, under that mysterious moving, a higher tone.

Faith in his fathers' God began to struggle within him for the mastery. Was he, a son of Abraham, the friend of the personal God, to sink down into the defiling superstition of Egyptian idolatry? Was he to forget the holy seed, and mingle himself altogether with the family of Mizraim? Was the bond that held him to his princely foster-mother as strong as that which bound him to the seed of Israel? So the Spirit of the Lord whispered to his inward ear, and he hearkened to it. "He went out unto his brethren, and looked on their burdens." The old hieroglyphics help us to realise the scene. In them we see fixed in yet remaining figures, the hard and bitter labours of the enslaved sons of Jacob toiling in the brick-field beneath their Egyptian overlookers, who are armed with rods of chastisement, and are exacting without pity the exertions which were designed quite as much to bow the spirit and even reduce the numbers of the serfs as to add to the riches of their masters.

It was a great and noble choice that he was led to make when he "refused to be called the son of Pharaoh's daughter, choosing rather to suffer affliction with the people of God than to enjoy the pleasures of sin for a season."

Herein, doubtless, that divine germ of faith, which was struggling for its birth within his great but as yet unpurged heart, was reaching forth far beyond his own consciousness. Already as it was read by the All-discerning Eye to which all things future are ever present, he was, like another great spirit after him, "counting all things but loss that he might win Christ;" for "he esteemed the reproach of Christ greater riches than the treasures in Egypt; for he had respect unto the recompense of the reward." No treasure cities, with all the countless stores which the magnificence of old kings had heaped up in them, could compare, in a soul once touched by God, with the possession of Him as its portion, to whom already, in all its darkness, its every aspiration pointed. Yet in that heart, chaotic strivings still wrought together with an undirected violence. There had been formed within it great volumes of power: he was thoroughly conscious of their presence; and as he mused upon the debased condition of his people, he felt himself impelled to be their deliverer. The breath of the divine impulse which fell upon him, mingled with, and for the time seemed lost in, the storm of a mere earthly ambition. Uncalled, uncommissioned, unstrengthened, he yields himself unconsciously indeed to the divine leading, but consciously only to the impulses of his own great heart. The favoured son of the servile race goes out from his palace ease and mingles himself with the sorrows of the oppressed. He has but a doubtful welcome. Slavery is an utterly debasing element in human life—debasing both to the master and to the slave. Fear, suspicion, jealousy, meanness—these are bred, as evil creatures breed in filth and darkness, in the slave's heart. They dare not, they will not understand their champion; and when he rescues even by violence a suffering brother from the tyranny of the Copt, and in doing the act of liberation with the inherited vehemence of a son of Levi, slays the Egyptian, he only awakes against himself the murmurs of his tribe, and is driven by their narrow-hearted and obstinate rejection of their prince to fly from Egypt.

That flight from Egypt had in it the elements of faith. For it was "by faith he forsook Egypt; not fearing the wrath of the king, for he endured as seeing Him who is invisible" (Heb. xi. 27). "By faith," beginning to teach him that not by his high place in Egypt, that not by his learning, that not by his power or might or resolution, but that by God's arm, in God's way, at God's time, the deliverance he longed to work, but had so failed in working, should be accomplished. He left the mighty unfulfilled design, which with too great human heat he had sought to accomplish, in the hand of God, and at the leading of His providence abandoned all his high designs to bury himself afar from all the stir of Egypt's life in the life of a wanderer and an exile. He seeks a shelter in the land of Midian amongst the Abrahamic tribes sprung from Keturah, and instead of the busy life of a courtier, a politician, and a tribune of the people, he associates himself to the pastoral pursuits of the dwellers on those Sinaitic ranges, which would support no larger animals than the flocks of their innumerable sheep. The natural sinking of that bounding spirit must have been profound. Hopes suddenly dashed; high desires burnt out and choked in the deadness of their own ashes; the sadness of separation from his brethren; the aimless uselessness of what he had dreamed of making a more than imperial life—all lay heavy on him. The name of his first-born son still mourns on our ear, charged with the record of this utter sorrow. "Zipporah bare him a son, and he called his name Gershom (Banishment), for he said, I have been a stranger in a strange land" (Exod. ii. 22).

Yet it was not all sorrow. It was a sharp discipline through which he was passing, but it was the discipline of God. We may even read its progress in the name he gives to his second son. There is a certain tinge of bitterness in the "Banishment" which breathes through the name of Gershom; but in Eliezer, the second, "My God is an help," we may measure something of what he had learned whom God was training. That fiery Levite spirit was being duly attempered; that longing to use for the redressing of wrong the arm of flesh was being curbed; that lofty estimate of what his natural powers, his high attainments, and his pride of place might enable him to accomplish, was being brought down to the far stronger basis of a self-distrusting humility. What a training it was:—with the half-stranger wife, unable even to the end to enter with wife-like sympathy into his deepest life and greatest hopes;—following the almost self-guided steps of the flocks of Jethro;—mounting with them as the summer heat increased from the lower valleys high up into the roots of the great peaks of that stony range;—listening to the unceasing voice of the crumbling rocks as in that silent air their roaring fall echoed through the stillness of the day; —communing with his own heart and with his God;—hardly daring to look back at the past, and having before him no revealed future; his life suddenly shut in by bars as close as those with which the ribs of the mountain closed the ever-narrowing valley! Had it been his own rash, impetuous zeal which had led to such an issue? Might he not have stirred to fiercer heat the Coptic jealousy and hatred towards Israel? Might he not by this uncommanded act of violence have put back their deliverance, and checked the present development of the merciful purposes of God for them? Dark thoughts like these, heavy-faced and threatening in their presages, would close in upon him in the waste places of the wilderness, and threaten to bow down utterly his spirit. What a discipline it all was; what a preparation; what a strengthening of the will; what a beating down of self; what a realisation of God! How in after years, when again he trod the same paths, but with the thousands of Israel to guide instead of the few sheep in the wilderness, must he have looked back on those days! How would every familiar mountain scene, with its marvellous power of imbibing and returning to us the long-past life, remind him of those years of meditation, prayer, and silence, and again and again amidst the murmuring of the stiff-necked people how must it have animated his fainting heart for new acts of faith, patience, and daring!

In the midst of this life which had spread its level, unvarying outline over forty years, the call of God suddenly aroused him. For four hundred years that voice had not, it seems, been heard within the chosen family. Since the death-bed of Jacob, prophecy had been dumb. The family of promise grew, multiplied, abounded, but no voice from God visited them, no breath of heavenly inspiration stirred the sleeping chords of their tribal being. In the wilderness of Midian, at the foot of that great mountain of Horeb which was to be hereafter "the mount of God," the old dry river-courses filled again with the heavenly stream; the old voice which had called Abraham, and directed Isaac and comforted Jacob amidst his many troubles, woke up to give his great commission to Moses. The strange sight of the thorn-tree of the desert, instinct with fire and unconsumed, at once invited the curious investigation of the man to whom Egyptian science had opened all the then known secrets of nature. "I will now turn aside, and see this great sight, why the bush is not burnt" (Exod. iii. 3). But as he draws near to gaze, a greater wonder than any which nature could display arrests his inmost spirit. Whether it was then given him to read the riddle of the sign we know not. Whether it was still to him but a burning bush, or whether in the dwarf thorn amidst the forest trees he read the form of suffering Israel, penetrated everywhere by the living fire of their fathers' God, purifying but not consuming the race He was searching with His judgments and upholding in His love—whether then or afterwards his eye read that parable of providence, we know not; but from that bush we know that the voice spake to him, called him by name; bid him put aside in humble adoration the shoes from off his feet, and filled him with such a sense of holy awe that he sank astonished at the manifested presence of the God with whom these forty years he had been walking. He whose educated gaze had known no fear in looking at the strange natural phenomenon of the burning, unconsumed thorn, trembled to the centre of his being at this revelation of the nearness to him of God; and "he hid his face, for he was afraid to look upon God" (Exod. iii. 6).

Then to that awe-struck spirit was given the commission which with mere earthly heat he had reached out his hand to seize some forty years before. Now the sufferings of Israel were accomplished. God had heard their groaning, and looked upon them, and had respect unto them (Exod. ii. 24, 25). What words of wonder embodying, what stores of consolation for all after-generations of suffering humanity, until the last task-master is cast out, until the last son of Abraham is made free of all his inheritance, until Egypt has given up to Canaan the last weeping exile, are those of the deliverer's commission!—"I have surely seen the affliction of my people—I have heard their cry, I know their sorrows" (Exod. iii. 7). This was the utterance of his fathers' God to him who long ago had dreamed of delivering his brethren. And now the dream was to be fulfilled. For now had come the moment for which the manifold discipline of a life prolonged to eighty years had all along been preparing him. He was passing through that great crisis which every life that yields itself consciously to God must in some mode or other experience. With him it was gathered up unto an awful suddenness of act and sharpness of feature. Doubtless he had known from a tradition, which four hundred years could not destroy, the being and the name of the God of Abraham. Doubtless, through his wandering in Midian, his spirit had been learning the secret of communing with its unseen Lord. But all this had been as the twilight to the sunrise. He had heard of his God by the hearing of the ear, but now his eye saw Him—the "I Am." The "I Am," the everlasting, self-existent, Almighty God, stood beside him; called him by his name; stood beside him a person by a person; manifested Himself by words of wonder, by signs of power, by revealed purposes of love. Moses passed through that awful crisis, and he was another man. The sage learned in all Egyptian lore; the great soul mighty in word and deed; the deep philosophic intellect furnished with all transmitted wisdom, trained in all school subtleties, practised by the often-handling of great affairs, ripened into mellowness by solitude, nature, and self-converse—these remained; but on them all had passed a mighty change. Just as there settles down upon the mountain's brow the wreath of the morning mist, investing every peak and pinnacle and crag with the glow and the glory of the molten sunlight which has drenched its folds, so on them had settled down the glory of the Lord, transmuting the earthly into the heavenly, raising the intellectual into the spiritual, making the man of power into the man of God, the noble philosophic patriot into the prophet of the Lord. His soul's eye had, indeed, seen the King, the Lord of Hosts. He receives at once his commission: and how different now from what it once had been is the voice of that trained heart! Instead of "supposing," uncommissioned, that "his brethren would have understood how that God, by his hand, would deliver them" (Acts vii. 25); now, even with the direct commission which interpreted to him and authorised all the long-cherished aspirations of his soul; with the "Come now, therefore, and I will send thee unto Pharaoh, that thou mayest bring forth my people, the children of Israel, out of Egypt" (Exod. iii. 10)—he shrinks back with a humbled sense of his own unfitness for being God's instrument. "Who am I, that I should go unto Pharaoh, and that I should bring forth the children of Israel out of Egypt?" The long training had done its work. The heated iron of his natural impetuosity had been hardened in those cold waters of his banishment, and the tempered steel was fitted for the mighty emprise for which God would wield it. The path by which he is led is wonderful even to himself. The name of God has been revealed to him: the promise of God's presence has been made sure; his bashful self-distrust turns into a growing confidence in his God; and at last, as one who trembles at the venture, and yet fears still more to disobey, he accepts the high commission, and prepares to be and do and suffer whatsoever the Heavenly Wisdom shall have ordered for him.

One other merciful assistance is granted to him before he is called on to endure the last appalling trial of his courage—his standing before Pharaoh. Having left his wife, with her children, at his Midianitish home, he sets out from Jethro's house, as forty years before he had come to it, a solitary man. But at the roots of Horeb he meets his elder brother Aaron, the future partner of his mighty cares. What a meeting it was! The great prophet lawgiver and the great high-priest of the future—with that gap of forty years in their lives to bridge over with long histories of the past, with the loving greetings of the present, with so much to tell and so much to hear, with such recitals of the wonders God had wrought already, such hopes from His great promises, such fears from the threatening aspect of the darkened sky, with its canopy of cloud, and all that it might contain for them in the unknown future. So they travel into Egypt, lonely wayfarers, with high resolves, with Egypt's and Israel's and the world's future waiting on their course.

How simple is all truest greatness! Here is

the whole record of that pregnant march: "Moses returned into the land of Egypt, and he took the rod of God in his hand" (Exod. iv. 20). "The rod of God"—what mysteries that name summed up! How did the presence of that rod mingle itself with all the chiefest wonders of the next forty years; with Pharaoh's chastisement and death, with Egypt's plagues, with Israel's passage through the Red Sea, with the overthrow of Amalek, with the feeding of the multitude throughout the desert march, with the water-springs which the rock of mystery should yield, with the prophet's greatness and his fall, with Israel's entrance into Canaan and the great leader's exclusion from it! Surely here are mysteries connected with that rod greater than all which legend has babbled, though it has well-nigh wearied itself in its stories of that sign and instrument of power; tracing it up to man's unfallen state in Paradise; recording its creation on the sixth day, its gift by God to Adam; bringing it with Adam through the gates of Eden as he passed a weeping exile under the flaming sword; and then carrying down the mystic gift through Enoch, Shem, Abraham, Jacob, and Joseph, to the house of Pharaoh; and thence carrying it with Jethro, then one of the king's chief magicians, to the wilderness of Midian, and so at last into the hand of Moses.

Thus he enters Egypt. The first work there is for the brothers to call together the heads of the family of Israel, and announce from God their coming deliverance. The suffering people hear with thankfulness that their God has remembered them, and "believe; and when they heard that the Lord had visited the children of Israel, and that He had looked upon their affliction, then they bowed their heads and worshipped" (Exod. iv. 31).

The next message of the prophet-messengers is to Pharaoh himself. Without reserve or fear they speak their summons, "Thus saith the Lord God of Israel, Let my people go." The king's reply is the natural answer of an irritated self-will to such a summons. "Who is the Lord that I should obey his voice?" At once, from those lately stammering lips of the messenger of the King of kings, the voice of a sovereignty asserting its supremacy far above the throne of the haughty Pharaoh, spake out its warning, "The God of the Hebrews hath met with us,—let us go, lest He fall upon us with pestilence, or with the sword." And now the strife between Jehovah's messenger and the great earth king was indeed begun. So far as Moses was concerned, it would have been ended in an hour, if Pharaoh had dared to drown the prophet's voice in his blood. But such an act was prevented by the state of Egypt. It was shaken to the centre by the power of the Canaanitish population which had settled in it. Between these and their brethren across the desert there was such a living sympathy, that every great movement of the one vibrated through the other. Fear of the power of Israel, should it join in one of the many insurrections which had raised and subverted the Mizraim dynasties, had first led to the cruel oppression through which they might be bowed and subdued. To provoke them to immediate rebellion by violence towards their chief would have been a dangerous policy. For they might be succoured by the Syrian tribes who still, as the seed of Abraham, retained some ties of affinity with the children of the eldest branch of their now wide-spread family. Pharaoh therefore spared the life of Moses, but sought to alienate the children of Israel from him by making their yoke heavier, so that they might rise against him as having by his interference only increased their sufferings. To a great degree the deep device succeeded. The suffering people groaned to their deliverers, "Ye have made us to be abhorred in the eyes of Pharaoh, and of his servants, to put a sword into their hand to slay us."

Here was for Moses the first experience of that utter unthankfulness in his brethren which so often in the forty years which followed made his life a burden to him. Yet this time so true was the complaint that he returned unto the Lord and said, "Wherefore hast Thou so evil entreated this people? Why is it that Thou hast sent me; for since I came to Pharaoh to speak in Thy name he hath done evil to this people, neither hast Thou delivered Thy people at all.'

To this intercession, as to so many afterwards from the prophet's mouth, the Lord hearkened; He renewed His promise: He raised the fainting spirit of His faithful servant, and He bared His arm against the persecutor.

Then began that series of ten plagues by which at the last Egypt and her king were bowed and conquered. They began, as all God's judgments do begin, in the muttered and distant thunder of the voice of warning; they passed next into the crash and peal of instant sentence: this, in its first execution, touched but lightly those who would not be warned; next it hemmed them round in ever-narrowing circles; until at last, in the death of the first-born, it closed indeed in blackness and desolation upon the very heart of Egypt.

Never once throughout this awful strife of the great earth king with the unseen Lord did His prophet faint or falter; contemned at first, then flattered and cajoled; then threatened, and at last driven with violence from the Royal presence, he, with a hand which never shook and with a voice which never trembled, stretched forth the rod of power and spake the word of judgment.

But when the conflict was over and the victory won, and Pharaoh and his host drowned in the depth of the sea, the trials of the great messenger rather began than ended. To lead forth indeed, as it was given him to do, a mob of slaves, debased as slavery only can debase humanity; sunk below the dead level of pagan Egyptian civilisation; to form them into a daring army, a free commonwealth, and a believing Church; to be exposed to all the ready and violent vicissitudes of their desires, and hopes, and fears, and so to have to suffer their manners in the wilderness; to have them upbraid him for their very deliverance when their sensual natures lusted after the flesh-pots of Egypt; to have them talk of stoning him when the wells were dry; to have them dispute with him for his command, and rebel against his rule; to have them break their covenant with Jehovah, and turn to the sacred calf of their old Egyptian oppressors—all this was such a burden as was never laid on any other. It was at times too heavy to bear: it was such that even from his deep-enduring, princely heart, when he "heard the people," in their grovelling sensuality because the heaven-sent manna was not flesh, "weeping throughout their families, every man in the door of his tent," it extorted the passionate cry unto the Lord, "Wherefore hast Thou afflicted Thy servant . . . that Thou layest all the burden of this people upon me? . . . . Have I begotten all this people that Thou shouldest say unto me, Carry them in thy bosom?" (Num. xi. 10, 11.)

Yet such had been his training, such was the grace given to him, that but once throughout these weary forty years of daily-renewed trial and vexation did his faith fail. Most full of warning to those less tried by uttermost temptation is the history of that one fall. It suggests to us how the peculiar taint of our fallen nature may linger on, with an unsuspected presence, ready on any unwatchfulness to break out. The ignorant idea of Moses, formed upon the mistranslation of a word, calling him the meekest instead of the most enduring of men, is in direct contradiction of the whole character set before us in the Pentateuch. Impetuous ardour, asserting itself in even ill-considered action, is evidently the basis of the character of him who set unsent about the task of delivering Israel, who slew the Egyptian, and put to flight the shepherds of Midian. The same character may be traced in his one fall. Under strong temptation his natural heat of spirit for once broke through the long-established control under which it had been brought. This is spoken of as the root of his offence. The ceaseless provocation of the rebellious people "angered Moses at the waters of strife, so that it went ill with him for their sakes: because they provoked his spirit so that he spake unadvisedly with his lips" (Ps. cvi. 32, 33). When anger ruled his heart, even his firm faith fainted. The people were mad with thirst. God had bidden him speak unto the rock before their eyes, and promised that at his word it should give forth the needful supply of water. But for once he distrusted the command of God. He had known before this that the rod of God could bring forth water from the rock. Merely to speak and call for the hidden springs was a new and a yet stranger act of power. He looked upon the wild faces of the angry people; he felt the general murmur rising into a roar of madness; he heard the fierce cry of the leaders, "Wherefore have ye made us to come up out of Egypt into this evil place, where there is no water to drink?" and for once his lion-heart sank within him. "What," unbelief whispered, "what if thou shouldst call, and call in vain?" And so, half doubting, and yet half believing, instead of speaking to the rock, he smote it twice with the rod, the power of which he had already proved. The faithful God would not forsake His servant even in that hour of his weakness. The waters in their deep spring-head obeyed the uncommanded summons, and gushed forth in abundance, and the people drank and were filled. But the sentence of the righteous Lord was spoken, "Because ye believed me not . . . . therefore ye shall not bring this congregation into the land which I have given them."

And so he, the greatest of the whole prophetic line, he to whom God spake as He spake to no other—he too fell. One only on the whole stalk

of humanity unfolded into the perfect flower;
one only, "the intercessor" for Moses, as Moses
interceded for Israel, could say to the Father,
"The Prince of this world cometh, and hath
NOTHING in me."

Of that one Righteous Man amongst all the
prophets, Moses was the chiefest type. The
voice of God Himself declared his pre-eminence
over all the prophetic line. "If there be a
prophet among you, I the Lord will make myself
known unto him in a vision, and will speak
unto him in a dream. My servant Moses is not
so. . . . With him will I speak mouth to mouth,
even apparently, and not in dark speeches, and
the similitude of the Lord shall he behold"
(Num. xii. 6—8). All the deep meaning of this
wonderful declaration it is impossible for us to
fathom. It was fulfilled when, on the summit of
Horeb, the cloud which shrouded the insupport-
able brightness of the Divine Presence, and out
of which came "the Voice" declaring the name
of the Lord, swept solemnly by the longing,
shrinking prophet. Then doubtless there was an
immediate manifestation to his spirit of all that

it was possible for fallen man to sustain of the majesty of God.

So, again, it was, in the long sojourn in the Mount; in that dwelling in the brightness of God's glory which left a lustre on his own countenance; in those mysterious communings in the separated tent, the entrance to which the pillar of the cloud had closed to all beside him, and where were given to him the separate directions of the law, as on the Mount, had been showed to him the patterns of the tabernacle worship. Language cannot rise above the words of wonder in which these last communings are described—"As Moses entered into the tabernacle, the cloudy pillar descended and stood at the door of the tabernacle, and the Lord talked with Moses. And all the people saw the cloudy pillar stand at the tabernacle door; and all the people rose up and worshipped, every man in his tent door. And the Lord spake unto Moses face to face, as a man speaketh to his friend" (Exod. xxxiii. 9—11).

A most fit emblem, moreover, was he of the one great Prophet, in his intercessions for

Israel,—intercessions based upon his renunciation of himself for his brethren. In all of these most descriptive lines of his figure, we may trace the forecast shadow of "that Prophet that should come into the world" (John vi. 14), of Him of whom the promise, which waited fourteen hundred years for its accomplishment, spake in the days of Moses to Israel—"I will raise them up a Prophet from among their brethren, like unto thee, and will put my words in his mouth" (Deut. xviii. 18). In the view of all this greatness, it is the direct record of inspiration, "There arose not a prophet since in Israel like unto Moses, whom the Lord knew face to face" (Deut. xxxiv. 10).

Here, as in so many other instances, we may note that the highest prophetic gift is not the mere predictive faculty (though that, too, played around the lips of Moses in his blessings and his songs), but the bearing the message of God to man; the being the witness to the fallen race of the presence, care, righteousness, truth, and love of the Almighty King.

Such a witness Moses bare for forty years

throughout the long wanderings of the wilderness, to that stiff-necked generation. He gave them Jehovah's law, he instituted for them their appointed worship, he lived before them the prophet lawgiver of Israel, he fulfilled his mission, and then the time came that he should enter on his rest. "Moses was an hundred and twenty years old when he died. His eye was not dim nor his natural force abated" (Deut. xxxiv. 7). What a life it had been, as the old man cast back that clear eye through its tale of years! That early rescue, that courtly sojourning, that grand mastery of the world's learning; those vast vistas of imperial greatness which had opened before his manhood's prime, to be consciously abandoned; that burning patriot-zeal, and its hasty, uncommanded outbreak; those long solitary exiled years; that growing commerce with his God; that crisis of the revelation to the spirit of Jehovah's personal presence; the struggle with Pharaoh; the great deliverance; the people's murmurings and strivings; the ever-renewed, ever-increasing communings with God, which kept his heart firm and his spirit faithful, amidst all the innumerable trials and troubles of his "much enduring" life (Num. xii. 3). He looked back upon it all as, a lone and solitary man, his feet began the last ascent of the mountain Abarim. The solitariness in which all great spirits are wrapped, was cast eminently around him. Miriam was long since dead. He had closed the eyes of Aaron when they had climbed together the Hill of Hor. Two only of all who had come with him out of Egypt survived—both still young men beside the aged prophet. One wish only of his heart remained to be accomplished, and that was denied him. He would fain have led the people into the land of their possession. But the word of the Lord had been spoken, "Get thee up into the mount Abarim, and see the land which I have given unto the children of Israel. And when thou hast seen it, thou also shalt be gathered to thy people as Aaron thy brother was gathered. For ye rebelled against my commandment in the desert of Zin, in the strife of the congregation." Meekly was that reverend head bowed to the

Will of God. One prayer only remained to be breathed up for Israel, "Let the Lord, the God of the spirits of all flesh, set a man over the congregation .... that the congregation of the Lord be not as sheep that have no shepherd" (Num. xxvii. 12—17).

And then began the ascent. Tradition, with its magnifying haze, has gathered round the aged man the weeping people, crowding round him for a last farewell, up to the mountain's base, the senate keeping him yet further company; the high priest, Eleazar, and Joshua, his successor, still talking with him as the cloud received him out of their sight (Jos. Antiq., Book II. cap. viii. § 48). But grander far is the simplicity of the Scripture narrative—written in prescience, as Josephus hands down the tradition—"Lest men should say because of his extraordinary merit that instead of dying he went to God" (Jos. Antiq., IV. viii. 48). In the record of the Book of Deuteronomy, he mounts alone at God's bidding, and with His sole companionship, from the plains of Moab unto the top of Pisgah. Thence the Lord showed him all the land, and said unto him, "This is the land which I sware unto Abraham .... I will give it to thy seed. I have caused thee to see it with thine eyes, but thou shalt not go over thither." And now, the last prayer breathed, his work done, the last sight seen on that mountain-top, far above the sounds of earth, the solitary man lies him down, in stillness and in light, to yield up to his Creator and Redeemer the great spirit which he had so richly trained through manifold discipline and unequalled heavenly communings. No hand of man closed those sinking eyelids; no tool of man dug that unknown grave, or traced over it an earth-born memorial. From first to last, God and he were alone together. "Moses, the servant of the Lord, died there in the land of Moab, according to the word of the Lord. And He buried him in a valley in the land of Moab over against Bethpeor, but no man knoweth of his sepulchre unto this day" (Deut. xxxiv. 5, 6).

Let us sum up his character and life in the words of another grand and ardent soul, subdued, like his own, by the marvellous dealings with him of the Highest:—"This Moses, humble in refusing so great a service; resigned in undertaking, faithful in discharging, unwearied in fulfilling it; vigilant in governing his people; resolute in correcting them, ardent in loving them, and patient in bearing with them; the intercessor for them with the God whom they provoked—this Moses—such and so great a man—we love, we admire, and, so far as may be, imitate" (Aug., *Cont. Faust.*, vol. viii. 162).

JOSHUA.

IT was a fearful burden which the death of Moses laid upon the shoulders of Joshua. Surely he must have watched, as no other member of the great Jewish congregation could have done, the beginning of that solemn ascent of the mountain of Abarim by the aged lawgiver of Israel. For the finger of God had already pointed him out as designed for succession to the perilous office of the leader of the people. "Take thee Joshua," had been the word of the Lord to Moses, "a man in whom is the Spirit, and lay thine hand upon him, and set him before Eleazar the priest, and before all the congregation, and give him a charge in their sight; and thou shalt put some of thine honour upon him, that all the congregation of Israel may be obedient."

That ascent of Abarim told him that the time was come when the long-looked-for burden must fall upon him. The circumstances of his past life had made him able too certainly to presage the toils and sufferings involved in the discharge of that great trust; for, beyond all others, he had been admitted into the closest and most peculiar intimacy with Moses; and he had seen, therefore, in the unreserve of confidential intercourse, how the great leader's heart had almost broken under the waywardness of his people. He had gone up with his master into "the mount of God" when the tables of the law were to be given (Exod. xxiv. 13). He had seen the great prophet enter into the enshrouding cloud (ver. 15). He had met him when he came forth from the glory, bearing in his hands the two tables graven by the very finger of God. His younger ears had caught first the confused sounds which rolled up the mountain side from the tented plain below, and with the interpretation of the uncertain noise most natural to a soldier, he had at once said unto Moses, "There is a noise of war in the camp." He had marked the clouding over of that countenance on which the heavenly radiance glistened, as the sternness of a holy indignation settled on its features. He had seen the righteous anger of the great prophet cast out of his two hands those precious tables of the law, and break them before the eyes of the offending people. Before this he had stood beside the vexed leader when the people were "almost ready to stone him" (Exod. xvii. 4). He had watched the agony of his spirit when he fell down in intercession for them; he had seen even his natural temper roused and his faith fail beside the waters of strife.

How could one who had known all this but tremble when the lot of God took him, and handed over to him the terrible charge of such a people? How could he hope to endure it? For he had not received the long and varied training which had fitted the great lawgiver to discharge so weighty an office. No knowledge of men gathered during a life's sojourning at Pharaoh's court; no deep training in

Egyptian learning; no long, lonely meditative wanderings amidst the grand Sinaitic mountains had been his. He was born a slave at about that darkest time, when Moses fled into Midian. His training had been that of his brother serfs in the brick-kilns, and under the taskmasters of Egypt. How should such an one as he become, in Moses' stead, the leader of his brethren?

Yet was there no escape for him. The mantle had fallen upon his shoulder, and where he was bidden there must he go. Through those thirty days of stillness, whilst the camp was full of weeping and mourning for Moses, he could revolve all these deep forebodings in his heart. But the days of inaction soon ran out their little span, and the Voice found him out in his tent, and spake to him the dreaded charge. "Moses my servant is dead; now therefore arise, go over this Jordan, thou and all this people, unto the land which I do give to them."

Though all natural misgivings made him shrink back from the charge, yet his high faith accepted it. Already, more than once, he had experienced God's power to aid him in his greatest need.

First, when at the earliest battle in which Israel was engaged with the chosen warriors of victorious Amalek at Rephidim, to him had been given the command of the untried army of Israel. Again, a second time he had himself known God's power to succour, when he and Caleb alone of all who were sent out to search the land did not, on their return, discourage the hearts of their brethren. The distinctive features of all his after life and character come out with startling clearness in the grand utterance of this, his early counsel:—"The land which we passed through to search it is an exceeding good land; if the Lord delight in us, then He will bring us into this land, and He will give it us, ... only rebel not ye against the Lord, nor fear ye the people of the land, for they are bread for us: their defence is departed from them, and the Lord is with us: fear them not." But it was to an unwilling audience that these grand words of faith were uttered, and they did but provoke the unbelieving wrath of the clamouring people. More dangerous than all their searchings of Canaan was that undistinguishing fury of the passionate multitude. "All the congregation bade stone them with stones." But even then, when the furious uproar of the people had swelled to its highest and most threatening tide, God interfered for His faithful ones; and "the glory of the Lord appeared in the tabernacle of the congregation before all the children of Israel" (Num. xiv. 10).

On these past deliverances in that hour of dread his spirit rested and stirred up its energies for the new venture of a life. Moreover the voice of God spake with loving warning and fatherly encouragement to those natural misgivings: "There shall not any man be able to stand before thee all the days of thy life; as I was with Moses, so I will be with thee; I will not fail thee nor forsake thee . . . . Only be thou strong and very courageous, that thou mayest observe to do according to all the law which Moses my servant commanded thee. . . . . This book of the law shall not depart out of thy mouth, but thou shalt meditate therein day and night, that thou mayest observe to do according to all that is written therein. . . . . Have not I commanded thee? be strong and of good courage; be not afraid, neither be thou dismayed; for the Lord thy God is with thee whithersoever thou goest" (Josh. i. 5—9).

All the after life of Joshua is the carrying out with a remarkable simplicity of unquestioning faith this first charge of his God. His obedience is immediate. The days of waiting are passed. There is no more sign of doubt or of misgiving. At once he assumes in all its breadth the office so committed to his hands, and as God's vicegerent "commands the officers of the people" (Josh. i. 10).

The first command was one which showed his great faith, and tested severely the obedience of the people. The river Jordan lay between the camp and the land of their promised inheritance, and it must be passed over by them at the very outset of their march. But how could this be accomplished? Even if it were possible, with difficulty and risk, to transport over it a chosen handful of warriors, how could he possibly carry over the mixed multitude—the women and the children, and the flocks and the herds? Even over the fords of Jordan, under the most favourable circumstances of the river, this would have been almost impossible; and at this season of the year, when, from the melting of the snow upon the highlands, Jordan was greatly flooded (for Jordan overfloweth all his banks all the time of harvest), it was more than ever impossible (Josh. iii. 15). Yet, down to these threatening floods, on the hopeless errand of passing over them, all the people are ordered to march Surely, it must have been a sore strain upon the simple faith of the young commander to issue such an order. But his faith was strong, and he commanded, and was obeyed. And then, as the first reward of such a holy confidence, the old promises on which his heart rested were made clearer and far more explicit than they had been before. "This day will I begin," the Lord his God promises, "to magnify thee in the sight of all Israel, that they may know that as I was with Moses, so I will be with thee" (Josh. iii. 7). Then followed the stupendous miracle: when the soles of the priests' feet who bare the ark of God touched the water's brim, the upper flow of the river was arrested and stood in a heap, leaving bare the river-bed. Into it the priests advanced until they reached its centre, and there they halted with the ark, which stood as a barrier to the descending waters, heaping them up as a liquid wall suddenly congealed in their fiercest sweep, leaving below a broad passage for the whole multitude to pass. From the river bed Joshua commanded one chosen man of every tribe to bear upon his shoulder a stone, to form on the bank a pillar of memorial; whilst he placed another, also of twelve stones, in the bed itself, where the priests' feet had stood on the dry land.

The river past, he stood at last with all the people in the true land of promise; and his first act on taking actual possession of the long-pledged inheritance was to renew the covenant of Israel with the God of Abraham by circumcising all who, in the license of the desert's wanderings, had grown up without passing through the appointed rite of initiation. Next they kept the passover: and then, as marking that the desert was indeed left for ever, the manna ceased, "and they did eat of the old corn of the land on the morrow after the passover" (Josh. v. 11). The next act was to invest Jericho, the great city of the valley of Jordan, and the key to all the passes which led up into the highlands of the land of promise. It was the greatest city of the Canaanitish race—beautiful in situation, girt on one side by a grand palm-tree forest; golden on another with the waving grain of "the barley harvest;" backed by the swelling hills which bounded it upon the west, and looking across the rich valley to the striking mountain range of Gilead. It was an emporium of the old world's wealth, and rich in wedges of gold, in shekels of silver, and in Babylonish garments. Its walls and its colossal gates could easily resist all assaults which any instruments of war then known could make upon them. It was "high and fenced up to heaven." It was too—as all great gatherings of the world's pomp, and wealth, and luxury unpurged by the fear of God must ever be, perhaps beyond them all—mighty in wickedness—a great festering sore of heathen abomination. Against this city, Joshua, with his men of war, set themselves. But it was not to be taken by their might. For seven days the ark of God is borne in solemn procession round it, and on the seventh, at the mysterious summons of the blast of the priestly trumpets, the mighty walls crumble and fall flat; the Israelites march in upon the city in the first spasm of amazement and terror which smote its inhabitants, and possess it thoroughly. Then at God's command, they destroy from off the face of the earth it and all that dwelt in it, except the household of Rahab.

These two marvels, both directly connected with the ark of Jehovah's presence, which had taken, as the symbol and instrument of His power, the place of the rod of Moses, were, of course designed at once to fill the heart of the Canaanites with that terror which is the forerunner of defeat, and to encourage the people of God to march on to all their after-dangers strong in their sense of His resistless strength. But there was yet another and, if possible, a still more difficult, lesson which this baring of the arm of God was meant to teach Joshua and them. The march of Israel was not to be a mere successful invasion. Joshua was not to be the general of a horde of earthly heroes who, to win for themselves a possession, were sweeping with fire and sword over the land of a weaker people. Unless every such imagination could be rooted out of their hearts, their very success would have been their utter ruin. With them, more even than with any other such invaders, this must have been the evil consequence of such a conquest. For that extermination of the Canaanites, of which they were to be the instruments, must have brutalised the executors of the sentence, unless they kept always clear before their eyes the reality of their terrible commission. Joshua could not have preserved that simplicity and gentleness which, side by side with a soldier's boldest daring, make up his character, unless all mere earthly feelings had been wholly overpowered by the sense that, as directly as the earthquake or the pestilence, he was God's simple instrument in sweeping from the earth a long-tried, long-endured, but incurably abominable race. These miraculous interferences were to teach him from the first that he was not as other "scourges of God" have been—the wielder of natural strength against natural weakness—the head of a race of men of larger stature, of braver natures, with habits unenfeebled by luxury and vice—who burst in their might, like the hurricane amidst the decaying trees of the sheltered forest, upon the soft slumbers of a worn-out people. This was the master truth of all Joshua's victories. He did not come as the leader of the Gauls or the Goths fell upon the degenerate Romans, who, before they yielded, trembled at the vast size and Titanic limbs of their strange invaders. The Israelites were the race of smaller stature. They were but lately slaves in Egypt; they had to confront the great and mighty sons of Anak; they were the unwarlike tribe; the people whose borders they invaded were men used to war and delighting in it. Though the Canaanites of the plain might have become effeminate and feeble, the Amorites and the other mountaineers were brave, hardy, daring, as well as vast in giant stature. Joshua's conquest was the victory of the weak over the strong, of the unwarlike over warriors; of the desert wanderers over horses and horsemen and chariots of iron. This was the lesson Joshua had from the first to learn. This great truth, as a talisman for his own safety, sunk into his spirit as he gazed on those heaped-up streams of Jordan and stood unshaken amidst the dust and din and terror of the falling walls of Jericho. He moved amidst these scenes of blood as an avenging angel might hover over them—a doer of the Will of the Holy One, untainted by human passion, and full, even in his most unswerving zeal for God, of a terrible gentleness. We read this character in his fatherly sympathy with the offending Achan, even whilst he condemned to be burnt with fire the great transgressor, who had brought himself and his under the ban of God. We read it in his faithful keeping of his oath to the men of Gibeon, when, because he had not asked counsel of the Lord, he had been deceived by their fraud. This it is all important, in dwelling on the history of the Book of Judges, to remember. For only in the spirit in which Joshua wrought them can we read aright his mighty deeds: and so read, they are rich in instruction which we most deeply need. We who live in these later days can see that the whole history of man hung upon the issue of those battles in the plain of Jericho and on the hills of Beth Horon. What other conflicts have ever decided so much for humanity? Joshua stood on those fields of blood the very world-hero, bearing with him all its destinies. If Israel had been subdued by the Canaanites, if the separated seed had been mingled with the heathen, if it had learned their ways, if the worship of Moab and Chemosh and Moloch and Astarte had superseded the worship of Jehovah, how had all the grand designs of redemption been frustrated in their development! The cry of Joshua after the flight at Ai would have been the despairing utterance of the race of men, "And what wilt Thou do unto Thy great name?" more almost in Joshua's history than anywhere besides, may the troubled soul—perplexed and harassed by the sight, on this sin-defiled earth, of wars, battles, slaughters, pestilences, earthquakes, miseries, and treasons —rest itself, though it be with the deep sob of a present broken-heartedness, in the conviction that God has a plan for this world; that in the end it does prevail; that the Baalim of heathen power must fall before Him, and that His Kingdom shall stand for ever and ever in its truth and righteousness and love.

But it was not only by these displays of God's might fighting their battles that the soul of Joshua was strengthened for his special work. This manifestation he shared with all the people who had eyes to read the dealings of Jehovah with them. But beyond others he had to bear the burden and heat of the day: he had to issue the fearful orders for extermination: he had to see them carried unflinchingly out to the utmost letter: on him pressed the whole brunt of temptation; and so to him were vouchsafed aids which others shared not. That same communication to his inmost spirit in the utter solitariness of his individual life which had been given to Abraham in his call, to Jacob in his desert wanderings, to Moses in the Wilderness of Sinai, was granted also to Joshua in his need. It was when he was "by Jericho;" whilst his eye was measuring those walls which fenced it up to heaven, whilst, it may be in the slant beams of the setting sun, he gazed with admiration at the grand proportions of its royal towers as they rose high in the golden light above, of its long fringe of majestic palm trees, of its glory and its wealth; and thought with awe upon the sentence which it was his destiny to execute upon every living thing within it—then it was that "there stood a man over against him with his sword drawn in his hand." Soldier-like, the captain-general demanded of him, "Art thou for us or for our adversaries?" The challenge woke at once the voice of Majesty. "Nay," not as thou deemest am I: prepare thy soul for God's unlooked-for visitation: "As Captain of the Host of the Lord am I come:" not as mingling with these earthly hosts; but as thy fellow in a higher order; as the Mighty ONE in heavenly places of whom thou art here and now on earth the type and shadow: as Him whom all the angels worship, as the uncreated Angel of the Covenant, as the Captain of the heavenly host of God have I come to thee. The soul of Joshua owned at once the presence of his God; "he fell on his face to the earth and did worship," and cried, "What saith my Lord unto His servant?" And then came the answer which the minister of Moses would read so readily in all the wide extent of its mysterious significance, the "Loose thy shoe from off thy foot, for the place where thou standest is holy." That burning bush of which his great master had so often told him in their solemn communings, must have risen before his eyes; and there was renewed unto him, with all the added awe of such a personal appearance, the earlier promise, "As I was with Moses, so also I will be with THEE." Yes, and far even beyond this; in his soul, as in the souls of the mighty ones before him to whom it had been granted thus to commune with the unapproachable Lord, there lay ever after resting on his spirit the shadow of that mighty intercourse hushing all lower sounds into an awe-stricken silence.

So strengthened from on high, he passed through those scenes of blood which were appointed for him, as the sun's ray streams untainted through polluted elements, until his mighty work of conquest was accomplished. Thus was he nerved for every battle. Under this influence he dared, when in the going down to Beth Horon the failing light seemed to threaten incompleteness to the decisive battle with the mighty Amorites, to raise his voice of high command above the eddies of the battle-field of Azekah, and in the name of the God of the armies of heaven to bid the sun stand still upon Gibeon and the moon in the valley of Ajalon. So he fought and so he conquered, until as the Eastern province had been before, so Western and Northern and Southern Canaan were all subdued by Israel and meted out by Joshua to its several tribes as the lot of God directed.

And now the ancient promise had been fulfilled: the solitary, childless patriarch who had listened to The Voice which spake at Ur of the Chaldees had grown by regular gradations into a family, a tribe, a horde, and now a nation. The inheritance of the heathen was theirs: wells they digged not, vineyards they planted not, cities they builded not—all these were theirs. Over the old strongholds of the mighty giant chieftains waved the banners of the House of Jacob. The brave single-hearted soldier had been enabled to finish thoroughly his mission. "And the Lord gave unto Israel all the land which He sware to give to their fathers, and they possessed it and dwelt therein .... there failed not ought of any good thing which the Lord had spoken unto the House of Israel; all came to pass" (Josh. xxi. 45)

Then, his work done, the great general retired to the lot which at the express command of God the grateful people had given him, and there he built on Mount Ephraim the city of Timnath Serah. There he dwelt in peace for some eighteen years of rest. We of this generation can understand perhaps more perfectly than most, how in those last years the grey hairs of the old conqueror and national deliverer were esteemed; how, long after his victories were all accomplished, his countrymen still felt safe in the enjoyment of their days of peace from the consciousness that the great chieftain yet lived amongst them; how they hung with admiring confidence on him who in his own person set ever before them the visible token of their God's past blessings to them. For to us, too, has it been given in the long years of peace which bitter war had bought, to look with ever-deepening admiration upon—

> "The statesman warrior, moderate, resolute,
> Whole in himself—a common good;
>   *   *   *   *   *
> Great in council and great in war,
> Foremost captain of his time.
> Rich in saving common sense,
> And as the greatest only are,
> In his simplicity sublime.
> O good gray head which all men knew,
> O voice from which their omens all men drew,
> O iron nerve to true occasion true." *

Yet the time came when Joshua too was to be gathered to his fathers. But before he passed away, one last solemn duty was yet to be discharged. He called together the heads of the people whom his arm had formed into a national life, left them his last charge, and bound them with his parting words to an everlasting cove-

* TENNYSON, "Ode on the Death of the Duke of Wellington."

nant of faithfulness to the God who had done such great things for them. How grand a gathering it was! There stood the victor in an hundred battles, now "old and stricken in age;" for it was already "a long time after that the Lord had given rest unto Israel from all their enemies." Before him was gathered all Israel, "their elders, their heads, their judges, and their officers," and he opened that mouth from which such words of might, and trust, and prayer had issued in the days of their troubles, and he spake to them what all felt to be his last counsels and commandments.

The words were still, as the great soldier's words had always been, instinct with the brief, stern eloquence of truth and action. "Cleave unto the Lord your God." "The Lord your God is He that hath fought for you" "Be ye very courageous to keep and to do all that is written in the book of the law of Moses: turn not aside therefrom to the right or to the left." "Put away the strange gods which are among you, and incline your heart unto the Lord God of Israel." "Take good heed unto yourselves that ye love the Lord your God." "Ye know in all your hearts and in all your souls that not one good thing hath failed of all the good things which the Lord God spake concerning you: all are come to pass." And then the voice died out upon their ears with that which woke a sob from many a rough breast, and dimmed many an eye with unbidden tears. Hard old soldiers who, in the fierceness of the Amorite battle, had looked at the spear-head which the then mighty arm had lifted and been strong, and heard that voice in its full volume and been nerved by it in the death struggle; who had seen the giant Anakim fall before him, and gained from his aspect courage themselves to play the man,—they sobbed at the sorrowful parting when the faltering voice of the old hero spake of his own departure from amongst them. "Behold this day I am going the way of all the earth."

Though his name is not written in the roll of the prophets, yet on him too rested the great Divine Indwelling. The mighty warrior, the true counsellor, the just divider, the strong and patient ruler; he too had partaken largely of the sevenfold gifts; he too left upon his people the mark of a great character and of more than earthly power. It is a grand record,—as of the trumpet's tongue when, dirge-like, it subdues its louder utterance only to witness more by its suppressed power,—"After these things Joshua, the servant of the Lord, died, being an hundred and ten years old, and they buried him in the border of his inheritance in Timnath Serah: and Israel served the Lord all the days of Joshua, and of the elders that overlived Joshua."

As on the dark sky, when some flashing meteor has swept across it with a path of fire, there remains still after that glory has departed a lingering line of light, so was it with this mighty man, glorious in life, and leaving even after he was gone the record of his abundant faithfulness still to hold for a season heavenward the too wandering eyes of Israel.

One other aspect remains to be glanced at of this mighty general. In more various points and with a closer similarity of outline than belongs, perhaps, to any other figure in the Old

Testament, is Joshua the type of Christ. His very name begins the great intimation. Changed by Moses—doubtless at the mouth of the Lord— from Oshea, "welfare," to Jehoshua, or Jesus, "God the Saviour;" it pointed him out as the figure in the earthly of the heavenly deliverer. Joshua moreover is pre-eminently one of the people whom he delivers; he has worked with them in the brick-kilns of Egypt, he knows their hearts; in all their afflictions he has been afflicted; and so Jesus stooped to be made in all points like unto His brethren, that, having been Himself tried with all temptations, He might know how to succour them that are tempted.

When Joshua has entered on his leadership, prophetic acts, full of typical significance, begin with a wonderful minuteness to repeat themselves. He and not the great lawgiver is to bring the people into Canaan: Moses must depart to secure his every word of promise being fulfilled to Israel, as the law must pass away and be fulfilled before the spiritual Israel could enter on their kingdom. At the river Jordan Joshua is shown by God to Israel as their appointed leader;

there God began to magnify him. As Jesus comes up from the river Jordan the heavens open, the Holy Ghost descends, and the voice of God declares, "This is my beloved Son, in whom I am well pleased." At Jordan's waters He too is declared to be given as a leader and a commander to the people. From Jordan's bed Joshua took twelve stones to be for evermore a witness to the people of their great deliverance; from His baptism in Jordan Jesus began to call His twelve Apostles the foundation-stones of that church which witnesses to every generation of the redemption of the sons of Abraham by Christ. Twelve stones Joshua buried under the returning waters of Jordan; and over the first twelve Jesus let the stream of death flow as over others; whilst they were repeated in their office of witnesses to Him by all the enduring succession of His earthly ministers with whom He is, even unto the end of the world. As soon as the chosen people, soiled by their long travel in the wilderness, enter the land of promise, Joshua renews in their circumcision the covenant of Jehovah's peace; and Jesus grants to all who pass the Jordan with Him the true circumcision of the Spirit. The Captain of the Host, as God reveals Himself to Joshua, is ever with the great earthly warrior of the people; and in the Man Christ Jesus dwells "the fulness of the Godhead bodily." The mighty walls of Jericho fall low as Joshua marches his appointed circuits around them, compassing them seven times with the ark of God's presence; and as Jesus accomplished His course the world citadel falls low; for unto the sevenfold gifts of the Holy Spirit yields the will of man; and the kingdoms of this world become the kingdoms of the Lord and of His Christ. Joshua leads the people of God into the promised land, but they must fight for their possession; and Jesus, though He brings His own into the spiritual Canaan of His church, has come not to bring peace, but a sword. Not one of His can sit down and dream his life away; each one has life's battle, earnest, hard, severe, to fight. As Joshua said of old to the children of Joseph, so to each one of His speaks our Captain, pointing to the hill of light and the everlasting inheritance, "Thou art a great people, and hast great power; thou shalt not have one lot only, for the mountain shall be thine." When his work was over Joshua mounted the hill of Ephraim and dwelt in his own possession, not falling to him as to others of his brethren by the lot, but as his own right yielded to him as the conqueror of all; and even so went up the Captain of our salvation to the heaven in which He was before, His own by right, His own by conquest. For "this Man after He had offered one sacrifice for sins, for ever sat down on the right hand of God; from henceforth expecting till His enemies be made His footstool" (Heb. x. 12, 13). Before Joshua departed, he called to him on that mountain of Timnath Serah which he was about to leave, all the heads of the tribes, and with the chant of a prophetic voice set before them all the grand future, which, if they clave steadfastly to God, should certainly be theirs; and so before He ascended into the heavens did the great Captain of God's spiritual army appoint to meet upon a mountain top in Galilee the heads of all the tribes into which His church should multiply, and there looking with them over the far outstretched dominions of the earth, did He utter to them, Joshua like, the words of wonder which rung for ever in their ears, "All power is given unto me in heaven and on earth; go ye therefore and evangelize all nations" (Matt. xxviii. 18, 19).

Yea, and yet again after a higher sort than belongs to this present world was Joshua but the type of Jesus. For it is He who for each one who follows Him, the true Captain of their Salvation, divides the cold waters of death, setting against their utmost flood even when that Jordan overfloweth his banks, as he doth all the harvest time, the ark of the body which He took of us, and in which God dwelleth evermore; so making a way for His ransomed to pass over. It is He who hath gone before to prepare amongst the many mansions of His Father's house the place which the golden lot marks out for us; it is He who hath trodden down all our enemies; it is He who hath built the golden city upon the "twelve foundation-stones, which bear the names of the twelve Apostles of the Lamb;" it is He at whose trumpet sound, when the seven days of the great week are accomplished, the walls of Babylon shall fall. It is He who goeth forth conquering and to conquer, until all His enemies are put under His feet; and so the last type of this life of wonders shall be fulfilled; and the true Joshua from the exceeding high mountain of His Timnath Serah shall look around Him on the tribes of God and see them all at peace; the prayer-promise which was breathed in time fulfilled in eternity: "Father, I will that those whom Thou hast given Me be with Me where I am, that they may behold My glory which I had with THEE before the world was."

SAMSON THE JUDGE.

THE last words of the great captain upon the slopes of Timnath Serah die out dirge-like in a tone of solemn sadness. The clarion note of his exulting praise ends in that uttermost foreboding, "lest ye deny your God." It was the shadow of the future which lay dark and heavy on that prophetic heart. For when "the generation which had seen the great works of the Lord had been gathered unto their fathers, another generation arose after them which knew not the Lord, and did evil in His sight. They forsook Jehovah, and served Baal and Ashtaroth."

Then were the days of gloom and darkness. Enemies rose against them on every side. The old mountain fastnesses of the giant brood frowned again like gathering thunder-clouds upon the habitations of Israel. The dark hosts of Philistia from their sea-coast dwellings, swarmed up even to the mountain slopes of Judah, and spoiled all the labours of the sons of Jacob. The strength of the separated race seemed to have spent itself in the act of invasion, and to have left them weak before the children of those whom they had subdued and dispossessed. And so in one sense it was; but not as the fruit of the natural wearing out of their energy. It was but the fulfilment of the voice of Joshua's departing warning. It was that "the anger of the Lord was hot against Israel, and He delivered them into the hands of spoilers that spoiled them."

Their peculiar sin was a direct and emphatic contradiction of the very purpose for which they were severed from the nations around them. Abraham had been called, Isaac blessed, Jacob guarded, Israel multiplied, that there might be one man, one family, one tribe, one people—to bear witness amidst the ever-multiplying polytheism to the indivisible unity of the Godhead

For the bearing of this witness it was above all things needful, not only that they should worship Jehovah, but that they should worship none other with Him. This was the sin of polytheism: it for ever multiplied its altars. From the deep of his own inner self-consciousness, from the play of his own imagination, from the shadows cast by outward things upon his spirit, fallen man developed his gods, until, not only every high hill and every dark forest, but every desire of his heart and every appetite of his senses was embodied in some deity, who repeated in gigantic proportions the sins which were his own defilement. Against this vast system of abominable idolatry, Abraham's solitary wanderings and his altars to Jehovah, Jacob's sufferings and visions, Joseph's captivity and advancement, the forty years of Moses amidst the mountain-chain of Midian, the thunders of Sinai, and the sword of Joshua, had all borne alike their various witness. To maintain this witness and to hand it on, Israel had been planted in the goodly land which, to make room for them, had vomited forth its old inhabitants. The adoption, therefore, by them of the Baalim and the Ashtaroth into their system of worship was a breach of their God-given charter—a yielding up of their title-deed to the land of their inheritance. Every mountain and valley, every rock and river lifted up to heaven their voices against this new pollution, and cried to Jehovah for deliverance from it. The cry was answered by the avenging bands of the Ammonite from his sloping hill-side, of the Amorite from his mountain fortress, and of the Philistine from his sea-girt plain. As the hands of Israel dropped Jehovah's banner their strength departed from them, and they became weak before their enemies. Internal disorganization, too, enfeebled them. Under their theocracy the heads and elders of the several tribes administered the earthly kingdom : they judged between man and man as the high priest judged between them and God, and so the separate families were held in unity, and the divided tribes felt flowing through them the blood of a common life. But justice and rule soon withered and died out beneath the sensual worship of the Baalim, and the disunited people fainted with the feebleness of internal estrangedness and ever-multiplying isolation. Then came the heathen forth as the bees of the forest from their hiding-places, and chased at will each lonely and defenceless wanderer. Then, at last, in their low estate they turned again to their God and wept before Him, and cast aside their idols and their Baalim. And their fathers' God hearkened to their cry and turned to them again.

But as the utterly relaxed sinews of their national existence were insufficient for the strain involved in rousing them again to make head against their enemies, the baring of God's arm called forth some unusual instrument through whom its power could act. Some one must be raised up with a might which rose above the withered strength of their ordinary institutions —who could breathe into their fainting hearts a new resolution, and gather into unity some at least of their disunited tribes. This was the judge's office. The choice of God marked him out. The hand of God separated him. The might of God strengthened him. He was raised up to do a special work, and he did it. He and his work must never be separated in our view, or we shall be sorely perplexed as we gaze upon him, and perhaps test and try to class him as though he were living and moving amongst ourselves. We shall never understand him by such a process; for God's witnesses and special instruments are never exempted from the influence of the circumstances which surround them. Through these circumstances God fashions and trains them. If it were not so they would be exceptional cases outside our sympathies, and could not be examples or instructors for us. The necessary effect of these circumstances is to imprint upon each one of them a specific and distinctive character. Whilst a strong common form of life thrown around men is a protection to the weak, it tends to diminish the strength of the strong. In the deep dark forest there is an almost unbroken uniformity in height and shape amidst its countless multitudes of trees. All are drawn up to the average size. But the mighty giants of the earth are found apart from their brethren; striking their own deep roots where they will, and flinging freely their vast branches to wrestle with every storm, and be nourished by every breeze.

Such were the judges of Israel; and we should therefore expect to find in them a certain eccentricity of act and character; the fruit of their largely developed individuality. So, in fact, they stand out before us; figures grand and majestic, but not of what we rightly consider a Christian aspect. There is upon every one of them, inasmuch as he was "a saviour" of his brethren, a shadowy outline of the one true Saviour of his people, but these lines which are so clear and true in him are broken, involved, indeterminate, confused, in them. As we trace them on the shifting misty medium on which we see the true image cast, to be distorted, even as it is repeated, they oftentimes perplex and turn us giddy as we gaze, unless we continually correct their strange and imperfect proportions by looking off from them to Him, the true type, whose perfectness redresses for us their manifold imperfections.

We, from the clear sunlight of Christendom, look back upon these judges, as men may look from a sunny bank over an intermediate valley on some ranges of distant mountains, amidst which, under their cloud canopy storms are breaking and sunlight is playing: whilst the separate hill masses seem like mighty giants at their sports or in their rest, on whom in their vastness we gaze with eager interest and rapt amazement.

In no one of the whole catalogue of the judges are all these distinguishing features marked with such startling clearness as in the Nazarite son of Manoah. Dark beyond all former precedent were the days in which he was born. East of the Jordan, the Ammonite had mightily oppressed Israel, until, in the time of Samson's youth, the Spirit of the Lord had fallen upon Jephthah, and raised him up for the deliverance of his people. In the west a yet heavier yoke had still longer bowed the people of Jehovah. For forty years they had groaned under the oppression of the Philistines, and the only fruit of attempted resistance had been to make the rod of the oppressor heavier, and the chains wherewith he bound them more galling. In their despair they took the ark of God into the battle-field, and took it there in vain. The battle was lost; the sons of the High Priest fell amongst the slain; the old man himself watching eagerly for the return of his Levite offspring, and more even than for them for Jehovah's ark, fell helpless from his seat at the announcement of the overthrow, and broke his neck. The curse had eaten out that evil progeny, and seemed through them to prophecy from the holy place a like destruction to the rebellious people round them. The infidel host carried off in triumph the captive ark, the great symbol of the covenant, the great instrument of worship. And still there was no voice, nor any that answered to their cry. It seemed as if, wearied out with their often-repeated iniquities, Jehovah had turned away for ever from His people. Not till the ark was placed as in triumphant subjection to the idol Dagon did the old power even begin to stir. Then the idol fell maimed and helpless on his temple's floor before the mysterious symbol of Jehovah's presence. Then upon the great cities of Philistia, wherever the ark rested, there were plagues, until the terrified heathen sent back their ark to their oppressed serfs. And now the same power began to stir in another quarter.

The portents which preceded Samson's birth pointed to him as a coming deliverer. We can picture to ourselves his wild and wayward youth. As self-consciousness dawned upon him, he found himself a Nazarite. Even before he was born the bond was upon his coming life. The angel messenger from God who had promised his birth to the barren household, had, in the might of a divine command, ordered that it should be so. As reason opened on that wilful soul, the story of his strange life was told him. With its earliest stirring was bound up the keeping of the mysterious vow. The growth of his unshorn locks, the abstinence from the familiar grape, the massive strength of his young frame, all severed him from others of his age— all stamped upon him a separated character. How must the father and the mother of the God-given, impulsive, solitary boy have gazed with something of an awe-struck wonder upon his moody youth! how must they have trembled at the dark violence of his passion, stirred often almost to madness, like the waves of the deep rock-bound lake, when the roar of the whirlwind lashes suddenly its surges into storm!

Was this the promised blessing? Could this be he who should deliver Israel? Yet at times that youth would be woke up to what seemed a promise for the future. He kept his Nazarite vow. With all his moody wilfulness, to that one bond he bowed. And when the rising fame of Jephthah's exploits found its way into Manoah's household, that dark spirit would stir as though the like influence were waking up it too to reach forward to do like acts of valour for his people; and they would look on, and wonder, and hope; for then "the Spirit of the Lord began to move him at times in the camp of Dan, between Zorah and Eshtaol" (Judges xiii. 25).

All along this history we can trace the broken outline of his typical character, as the image of The True Man is forecast upon this uncertain mist-blurred mirror. There was the angelic heralding to the childless parents of the coming birth of Israel's deliverer; there was the mystery which lay broad upon his youth, as "the child grew and the Lord blessed him;" there was the consciousness in that mother's heart of her guardianship of such a chosen life; there were those movings of the Spirit, which, with the promises "she kept within her heart," gilded with a light from Heaven the ordinary appearance of his up-growth.

The years rolled on. The boyhood and youth of Samson, with their strange fantastic promises and disappointments, had passed, and he was a man. "Surely now at last," the longing parents would say one to another, "surely now at last we shall see some fulfilment of the words of Him 'whose name is secret' (Judges xiii. 18), as to the Nazarite boy; surely now at last he will 'begin to deliver Israel out of the hand of the Philistines.'" The mother's brooding nature would instinctively move her to deal with Samson as a greater than Manoah's wife dealt with her greater Son, when, with longings which well-nigh swelled into reproach, she said unto Him, "They have no wine." But his hour was not yet come. What a strange mockery of their hopes must the first act of his manhood have seemed to them!—"He went down to Timnath, and saw a woman in Timnath of the daughters of the Philistines; and he came up and told his father and his mother; and said, I have seen a woman in Timnath, of the daughters of the Philistines, now therefore get her for me to wife" (Judges xiv. 1, 2). Used as they were to his wilfulness, this was beyond all the precedents of his youth. With eager entreaty they besought him to give up the misplaced alliance—"Is there never a woman amongst the daughters of thy brethren, or among all the people, that thou goest to take a wife of the uncircumcised Philistines?" But they spake in vain. His only answer was, "Get her for me, for she pleaseth me well."

Yet the strange choice was really the providential overruling of what in itself was faulty for the fulfilment of God's secret purposes. Samson's vocation was altogether peculiar. He was not to be the commander of an army. The depression of years had so utterly degraded Israel that her sons were not fit for such an enrolment. Neither was he to break the yoke of Philistia. His wild, wayward, sensual nature forbad that honour being his. He was but "*to begin* to deliver Israel out of the hand of the Philistines." He was to show by supernatural strength and individual daring that the power of God, if it were but called out, would abundantly suffice to overcome the Philistines; and yet that the might which at one time enabled him single-handed to scatter the hosts of the uncircumcised ebbed utterly away so soon as he departed from his God. This was the lesson Israel needed, and only thus could it be taught them. If the alternations of wonderful success and bitter casting down which marked his single course had befallen the armies of Israel, there could have been no recovery of their spirit of self-reliance, or of confidence in their God. But in Samson the great scene with its most tragic conclusion could be acted out before their eyes; and whilst his success elevated their hopes and roused their confidence, his casting down taught them its most needed lesson of warning, and yet left their rising spirit unshattered. He was as it were the embodiment of the chosen people; they could see themselves in him. His Nazarite condition represented faithfully their covenant state; his clinging amidst all his aberrations to that vow; his under voice of confidence in God; his perception that he had a vocation; a mission from Jehovah: his unshrinking daring in carrying it out by the matchless might with which the Most High had strengthened him; his well-nigh incredible success so long as he clave to this; —all this was to teach them that if they would cast off their Baalim and return unto their God, and cleave to Him, they would break in Jehovah's might the yoke of Philistia. His yielding to the voice of sensual appetite, with all the misery it brought upon him, was to show them in an example acted before their eyes that if they yielded to the sensuality, which was the great inducement to their idol worship, and joined themselves to the sins of the nations round, they too, like their hero in the arms of Delilah, would be snared, and blinded, and destroyed.

This then was to be Samson's service; thus was he to begin to deliver Israel out of the hands of the Philistines. He was not to break their yoke, but he was to show the trembling people that before the faithful man their strength withered and faded; and thus he was to keep alive in fainting hearts the hope of Israel. They were to see in him the tide of prophetic power ebb and flow as he claimed or denied his true relation to Jehovah. But to make this possible it was essential that he should have such relations with the oppressing heathen as would lead to their perfidy, and cruelty, and contempt, venting themselves upon him personally so as to embroil him with them, and thus make it natural for him in maintaining his own personal rights to avenge the oppression of Israel. For no single man could make war upon a nation. In this sense only Samson's wild choice of a daughter of Philistia for a wife, because she pleased him well, was "of the Lord." The act was a forbidden one. The motives which led Samson on to it were wilful and sensual; but his fault was to be overruled for the carrying out of the purposes of God. His father and his mother saw but the evil of the heathen marriage, and so resisted it whilst they could, and then, according to their wont, yielded to the stronger will of their imperious son. They go down to Timnath with him to get for him the Philistine damsel to wife. By the vineyards of the city a young lion springs upon him with that roar which shakes the forest; but alone, single-handed, and unarmed, he seizes it and tears it asunder, as if it were a kid, and does not even tell his parents of the feat

Here again how strangely does the typical character of all his acts of greatness float before us! His first recorded work of superhuman strength, yet wrought as man, alone and unarmed, as he goes down to begin his life-long fray with the Philistines, is this overcoming of the lion. And He, too, the One True Man, as man, immediately before the opening of his ministry, is driven of the Spirit into the wilderness to be tempted of the devil; to meet as man, alone—left for the time even by the bands of angels who, when the conflict was over, returned to minister to Him—the roaring lion who seeketh whom he may devour; to meet him and to overcome him in the might of the indwelling Spirit.

When Samson and his parents come to Timnath the damsel is formally demanded and betrothed to him as his wife; in due time he goes down again to claim his bride. The marriage festival is celebrated with great preparation and display, thirty Philistine children of the bride-chamber attending to do honour to their friend.

Again the strange similitude looks out upon us from the marriage banquet. For as it was at a marriage in Cana of Galilee, where first the power of the Son of Mary was miraculously manifested, so from the Timnath marriage feast came first the display of Samson's might against Philistia. Amongst the entertainments of the festival, according to the common usage of Eastern and even of Grecian feasting, Samson puts forth a riddle to the assembled guests. Philistian guile extracts dishonestly the answer by threatening to burn with fire the household of the bride unless she entices for them his secret from her betrothed. That hero heart of his, so strong against man's violence, so weak before woman's art, melts under her tears, and she gains and betrays his secret. Then there fell on him, as when the lion roared against him by the vineyard of Timnath, the burst of a divine wrath. He saw the perfidy, the darkness, the godless injustice with which Philistia was oppressing Israel, and he goes down to Askelon and slays thirty of its chosen men, and brings their spoils to pay the wager which had been so basely won.

This Philistian perfidy had brought the marriage festival to an untimely end, and Samson returns in wrath without his betrothed wife into the land of Dan. By degrees, however, his anger cools, and he goes down again to Timnath to claim his wife. He is met by a new instance of Philistian faithlessness. For he finds his wife given to his companion, whom he hath used as his friend. This new insult he avenged by turning three hundred of the jackals, who even to this day infest in numbers the neighbourhood of Gaza, tied tail to tail, with a lighted firebrand between each, into the standing corn of the Philistines, who, when they had ascertained the cause of their loss, came up with savage violence and burned with fire the house and family of Samson's bride. The language of the authorized version would suggest that Samson considered even that an insufficient punishment for his Timnite father-in-law's treachery. But the original language implies the very opposite. It suggests that his soul revolted from this abominable barbarity; and that he resolved to punish wholesale: "If ye do such things I will not cease until I have been revenged on you," would be the truer rendering. Then he smote them hip and thigh with a great slaughter.

It was after this act of heroism that he appears to have openly assumed the judge's office. He went down and dwelt in the cleft of the rock Etam, and there the people of Judah came to him for judgment. Yet his hold on his countrymen was as yet small. His acts of vengeance on the Philistine people stirred up, as he doubtless expected they would, the bitter anger of those national enemies. They gathered their troops together and invaded the territory of Judah to seize the person of the terrible Danite. The conduct of the men of Judah exhibits in the strongest light their utter national degradation. Instead of gathering around their judge, and even if their unarmed and undisciplined multitude could not stand in battle against the hosts of Philistia, yet seeking to strengthen his heroic heart by their sympathy, whilst they watched for what their God would do for them by his hands, they resolved to purchase an ignominious peace by the base surrender of their champion.

Again there breaks out upon us the recurring prophecy of act. For so it was generations after, in their children's days, when the Mighty One came unto His own and His own received Him not; when the evil murmur was whispered, "If we let him thus alone .... the Romans shall come and take away both our place and nation" (John xii. 48). "Knowest thou not," said the three thousand men of Judah to Samson, when they came to him at the rock of Etam, "that the Philistines rule over us? Wherefore hast thou done this? We have come down to bind thee, and deliver thee into the hands of the Philistines." Out of the ages comes forth as the accursed echo of that voice of faithless fear: "We have no king but Cæsar." And like acts followed in each case: "When they had bound Jesus they led Him away, and delivered Him to Pontius Pilate the governor." Even so did the men of Judah bind at Etam their Nazarite champion with two new cords, and brought him up from the rock. Both of the betrayed suffered themselves to be bound, because in those bonds they read the present Will of God and the road to a future and more complete victory; and the bonds of each were indeed the loosing of the prisoner's chains. So it was in the spirit world with the Captain of our salvation. So it was amidst the dark hosts of Philistia with the hero judge of Israel. "For when the Philistines" in triumph "shouted against" their captive enemy, "the Spirit of the Lord came mightily upon him, and the cords that were upon his arms became as flax which was burnt with fire, and his bands loosed from off his hands; and he found a new jawbone of an ass, and put forth his hand and took it, and slew a thousand men therewith" (Judges xv. 15).

Then in the moment of his triumph came to him to teach him his weakness without his God the sore thirst under which his mighty strength fainted. It was the time of wheat harvest, and as single-handed he fought the battle and destroyed the army of the alien, the sun of Judea poured down its scorching midday rays upon him until it seemed that he whom the Philistine hosts could not subdue would perish in the agony of drought. He cried unto the Lord in a prayer which witnesses in its every word to his deep sense of his being in these acts no mere pursuer of personal vengeance, but in very deed an instrument in the hand of Jehovah for the rescuing of His people. "Thou hast given this great deliverance into the hand of thy servant, and now shall I die for thirst and fall into the hand of the uncircumcised?" He did not cry in vain, for in the rock at Lehi He who bringeth water out of the great deeps opened its fresh springs, and when the thirst-bound hero had drunk, his spirit came again and he revived;

and in grateful remembrance he named the spring, which for years afterwards distilled its freshness from the rock of Lehi, "the spring of him that cried." As we read of this extremity, this prayer, and this deliverance, can we forget an agony in the dark strife of the Captain of our salvation far more terrible, a prayer far more mysterious, and a succour yet more wonderful, when "there appeared an Angel from Heaven strengthening Him?" So over and over again, as we look deeper into the record, does the Nazarite judge prefigure the true King of Israel.

Great at this time was the glory of Manoah's son. Terrified by the utter failure of their last attempt, the Philistines withdrew themselves into their own borders. Samson judged his people, and though the heathen yoke yet dishonoured Judah, it was little more than an empty token of subjection whilst Samson was at hand to avenge upon their trembling hosts any act of aggression or of wrong. For twenty years it seems that this long pause lasted, and then the last and greatest of the judges falls before the temptations of the flesh, and ends in shame and ruin his life of bright but fitful splendour. It is a dark and miserable history, to be told in a few mournful words, to be stored up by all for closest self-application in their heart of hearts. The mighty man "who had burst the fetters of his foes could not break the cords of his own lusts" (St. Ambrose). He yields himself up to the enticements of the evil and treacherous Delilah. The lords of Philistia seized greedily on the hope which this weakness of their great enemy suggested to them. They promised the woman large rewards if she could win from Samson the knowledge of the hidden abode of his great strength, which, according to popular belief, they supposed to rest in the possession of some amulet or charm, of which if they could rob him, they might afterwards securely bind and oppress him who had been their scourge and was still their terror. With the perfidy of her class, she uses all her harlot wiles to draw from him the coveted secret At three different visits he deceives her with fabled inventions. Once the sleeping giant is bound by her with undried thongs; once with new cords; once the Nazarite locks are woven together by her into one; and each time he is startled from slumber by the sudden cry, "Philistines upon thee, Samson!" Each time the awakening man manifests in a moment his unabated might, and his enemies, whom the cruel traitress kept hidden by her in the dark ambush of her chamber, dared not show their unsuspected presence. Then the attempt would be treated as an idle jest, such as frequent those chambers of iniquity. For evermore has existed the deadly conjunction which our own Milton's words of matchless strength have in almost a syllable so abundantly depicted—

"Lust hard by hate,"

and so his suspicions would be lulled to sleep, and it would seem to be but a woman's curiosity in one of its unmeaning sports with her victim.

But his last revelation, though it concealed the truth, had come dangerously near to its sacred secrecy. He had dared to sport with those seven mysterious locks upon his head, which were the outward sign, the mysterious sacrament, of his strength. This free and dangerous handling of the veil drawn over the hidden secret on which depended the indwelling of the power of Jehovah foreboded all that followed; and it needed but another wearisome solicitation, another passionate entreaty, another sportive guile, to draw from him all the truth, and place him helpless in the cruel hands of the deceiver. This time she saw that he had told her all his heart, and she sent with triumphant expectation for the lords of her evil people. Then as Samson slumbered in the sleep of sin, the razor passed upon his head. The Nazarite locks were shorn, the birth vow was broken, his separate state was ended, the special presence of Jehovah had departed from him, he had become as another man. Then again the cry rang through the chamber of sin, "Philistines upon thee, Samson," and he rose with his dishonoured head, saying to himself, "I will go away, as time upon time." He had come from long familiarity with its accesses to deem of the strength vouchsafed to him as if it belonged to himself. But he knew not that Jehovah was departed from him. Then from their secret hiding-place rose up the ambush of his enemies; the dark forms cast themselves upon him, to be received at first with his accustomed scorn. Then came the fierce death-like struggle: the mighty man accustomed to his strength could not believe that it was gone, and yet it was in very deed departed, and he is overmastered, bound with fetters of brass, his eyes put out—that last terrible security taken against any return of his might—and he is led away a captive to Gaza. There he is cast into the dungeon and forced to do the hardest work of the meanest drudges, to grind corn in the mill.

What must have been the thoughts of that great self-willed heart; what the agony of that mighty spirit; what the pangs of that rebellious body! How must the caged eagle have beaten its mighty wings against the cruel bars of its narrow cage! how must Israel's deliverer have groaned under the insults of the Philistines! how must Jehovah's champion have abhorred the triumphs of the infidels!

Doubtless in that prison the work of God

which he had so often counteracted was wrought indeed with him. Doubtless, in those lonely hours of darkness, with no familiar voice to cheer their blackness, with no sound of kindness to mingle with their gloom, conscience would arouse itself in all its might; doubtless he who needed so severe a discipline of love for his perfecting, had grace given him to yield himself to all its cleansing, purifying power; for his name, by the hand of God the Holy Ghost, has been engraven in the golden catalogue of the faithful; doubtless he, beyond all others, now that his earthly strength had departed from him was, in the higher sense of the great words, "out of weakness made strong."

The days, the weeks, the months, perhaps the years, passed on—passed in the slowly achieved conquest of his will to the Will of God—and down in the dark hold of the heathen dungeon, in his blindness and his squalidness, angels visited the lonely man, nay, the God who had made his Nazarite strength so strong was with him in the prison.

At last the day of his deliverance dawned.

The great feast of Dagon, the chiefest of the idols of Philistia, was come. He was the god of natural power—of all the life-giving forces, of which water is the instrument; his fish-like body, with the head and arms of man, embodied this idea of his rule. Sacrifices were this day to be offered to him; and amongst the chiefest of his honours, the great judge of Israel—the warrior who had been filled with all Jehovah's strength—was to be led forth to do the idol honour and exalt by his feats the delight of assembled Philistia in their hideous, misshapen God. The vast hall is full from end to end of Philistia's nobles; the flat roof crowded by the swarming multitude. Amidst the taunts and triumphs of a brutalized heathendom, the eyeless captive is led in. He is guided to the central columns, that all may the better gaze upon this living trophy of their triumphant god.

Amidst all that thronging garrulous crowd he is alone with his God. Blindness, sorrow, captivity, and loneliness have done their work upon the solitary man. All his great soul is turned inward. He scarcely hears or sees anything around him. His thoughts are with the past; with the days of his Nazarite youth; with his early associations; with his witness for his God; with his wanderings from Him. What is there yet that he can do, what is there that he can suffer, for that Lord? There is but one last offering he can make; it is the offering of himself: he is again in outward form a dedicated Nazarite. Has the God in whom, he now has learned, was all his early strength—has He come to him again? Will Jehovah accept even from one stained as he has been the offering of his all? He puts forth out of his deep heart the cry for one more gift of strength whereby the cruel sacrifice of his own eyesight may be avenged, whereby the enemies of Israel may be humbled, wherewith Jehovah may yet triumph over Dagon. He prays his last prayer; offers to his God his life; grasps with those arms of iron the massive central columns which support the wide-spanned roof, and bows himself with all his might. There is a shaking of the pillars; a cry of terror upon this side and on that—a wild rush beginning, and on it all settles down, with one loud crash mingling like the deep thunder with the cries of the dying, the vast proportions of the crumbling building. At last Jehovah has triumphed. Dagon has fallen before the God of Israel. The Hebrew judge has indeed wrought the destruction of the Philistines; the eyeless captive has done more than Samson in his might. "The dead which he slew at his death were more than they which he slew in his life."

Once again, for the last time, from amongst the dark shadows of his fall and ruin, which seemed for ever to shut out the glory of his prophetic character, the typical similitude is seen to re-awaken, and the hero judge bowing willingly his soul to death that Jehovah may be magnified and Israel delivered, foreshadows to us the offering of himself by the Great Judge of all unto the pains of death, that through death He might destroy him that had the power of death, that is, the devil, and deliver them who through fear of death were all their lifetime subject to bondage; and as the body of the

Lord was not left in the grave of the wicked, so is it expressly written for us, that the body of the Nazarite judge remained not with the uncircumcised amongst whom he fell, but that profiting, no doubt, by the first terror of that great overthrow in the temple of Dagon, "his brethren and all the house of his father came down and took him and brought him up and buried him between Zorah and Eshtaol, in the burying place of Manoah his father" (Judges xvi. 31).

As we look back upon this history with its intensely dramatic character, its wild lights, its strange incidents, its glories and its shame, gathering themselves round the hero chief, who evermore fills the foreground of the picture, we can scarcely resist the conclusion that the Hercules of pagan story was but the Samson of the inspired record distorted and robbed, by the thick vapours of the heathendom, of the moral teaching which breathes everywhere from the history of Manoah's son. There is the same exaltation of personal strength to an heroic nobleness, there is the same slaughter of the lion, the same single-handed scattering of his enemies, the same subjection of the hero's strength to the weakness of his own lusts, the same bowing down of his might before the witchery of woman's wiles, the same deceived end and premature death at the hands of the enchantress. But in Hercules man's appetites are deified, in Samson they show in undisguised harshness all the cruelty of their murderous outlines as the mighty man in his moral weakness allows himself to be cast down upon their rugged pinnacles.

This lesson, which lies upon the surface of this wonderful history, none can fail to read. The Nazarite separated to do the Will of God, strong against every foe so long as his vow, talisman-like, endures with him unrenounced; but falling through the weakness of the flesh; then led on deliberately to tamper with the very condition of his separation; then, partly by half consent, and partly by the fraud of the enemy, stripped of the very sign of his relationship to God; finding, too late, that God has departed from him, and with God the strength which, in his self-confidence, he supposed would still be with him as at other times; then bound by the enemies with whom he had tampered, cast into their dungeon a blinded, manacled slave, or led forth to be the sport of their bitter and triumphant hatred—all this is the story of each Christian castaway, seen through so transparent a veil that we cannot fail to mark in it the typical outline of a baptism into Christ, with all its separating power, with all its spiritual might sacrificed for the lusts of the flesh, abandoned at last even in profession, and leaving one of the mighty ones in the prison-house of darkness, blinded, manacled, and utterly enslaved, the sport and mock of those evil enemies who crowd around their accursed chief in the dungeons of the lost.

But this is not the only lesson of this startling chapter in the book of inspiration. The ever self-repeating action of humanity and the many-sidedness of God's Word—every facet of the mighty whole darting forth its own separate gleam of light upon the mystery of being—make it read to us perhaps a deeper moral still!

We may see in it how those who for the highest purpose have been endowed with the highest gifts, on whose intellectual powers that mighty spirit of God's strength has rested, that they may work some deliverance for His people, may idly throw away, first, their noble trust, and then, at last, themselves. Samson's gifts of bodily strength, which were the consequence in him of the Spirit of God exalting the ordinary powers of man's muscles and sinews into the heroic might of the Nazarite deliverer, are a type of the quickening of the higher gifts of intellectual power by the informing Spirit into a grander reach of exertions than the merely natural mind could have attained. The employment of these at the mere bidding of the selfish will, for sport, for gain, for the gratification of a vain daring, for the pleasure of unbridled speculation, is the fulfilment in a higher sphere of the casting away of the sensual, wayward judge of the tribe of Dan. His end is a type of the yet greater fall of these worse abusers of higher gifts. They, too, when they have sold their Nazarite locks at the bidding of the enchantress, when they have trifled with the gifts of the Holy Ghost, which were theirs in the Church of the redeemed, hear from the lips of that goddess of unsanctified reason, on whose lap they are dreaming, the startling cry of "Philistines are upon thee, Samson!" and in that crisis such men find, as he did, their strength departed. They are bound with the cords of doubts, plunged, often blindfold, into the dungeon of despair, to grind out for the world all her baser problems, to feed her godless company of scoffers. Happy were it for such if even by the sacrifice of a life they could pull down the temples of unbelieving thought upon the crowd of blasphemous imaginations which cling to and throng around them.

SAMUEL THE PROPHET.

WHILST the troubled life of the Danite judge was running out its wild course, another Nazarite from the womb was growing up in Israel under other influences and with a far different destiny before him. He, too, was given to a long barren mother, in answer to the cry of her half-broken heart. Deep sorrow had, through the grace of God, wrought in her its true work, and brought her to cast herself, with all her cares and oppressions, at His feet. In every sense of the words, Samuel was given to her prayers. Given in his natural life; given, too, —as St. Augustine was given to the prayers of Monica, and as so many saints besides have one by one been given,—in his spiritual life, to the cry of her heart to her God. She herself practised the abstinence from wine and strong drink which formed so large a part of the Nazarite vow, and she devoted the child for whom she prayed, not only to bear from his birth the ordinary obligations of a Nazarite, but also to render to the Lord a life-long service. Accordingly, when he is three years old, she brings him up to the sanctuary at Shiloh, and leaves that precious life with the high priest Eli. There that holy childhood grew on, fed by the special dews of the blessed Spirit. Every opening faculty of his young heart was thus from the first consecrated to God, whilst with childish blamelessness, girded with a linen ephod, he ministered in the sanctuary by day, and lay down within its precincts to sleep at night.

Great and pregnant with mighty issues was the life which was being thus guarded. In him the line of the judges was to end, in him the mysterious catalogue of the prophets was to begin. It was a great crisis in the dealings of God with His people. They were to be recalled to Him, to be roused out of their apathy and spiritual deadness, to be consecrated anew to Him. They were to be delivered from the yoke of their oppressing enemies; their national life was to be developed; they were to be consolidated into a kingdom, instead of being held loosely together as a congeries of tribes.

To meet the needs which this new development of national life must create, the prophetic office was called into being. The throne of the King of Israel was to have beside it this special honour, that one should be ever near who could speak the utterances of Israel's God. For reproof, for direction, for counsel, that voice could ever be awoke. To Saul, to David, to Solomon, to Rehoboam, to Hezekiah, to the founder of the northern kingdom, and to his successors, we hear it from time to time speaking its solemn, its alarming, its consoling accents. It is ever present as a real abiding power to the kingdom's end; dying out, at last, in the sad wail of Jeremiah's lamentations.

For this office in its earliest, and, in some respects, never equalled strength, Samuel's youth was training within that shelter of the tabernacle at Shiloh. Those were dark days with Israel. The tribes had, one and all, wandered far from Jehovah, and yielded themselves up to the abominations and impurities of the heathendom around them. They chose new gods; then was war in their gates. And in those wars they were continually worsted; until the Philistines had brought them so utterly into subjection that they had almost ceased to rebel against the yoke of their oppressors. Samson in the west, and Gideon in the east, had indeed, in some measure, rebelled against this evil domination, and whispered some hopes to the downcast heart of Israel. But they had wrought no enduring deliverance for their people. To work such an emancipation far more was needed than the mere overthrow of their enemies. Israel's subjection was the fruit of Israel's sin; and the heart of the people must be brought back to Jehovah before they could break the heathen yoke asunder. But whence was this deliverance to come? It could not come from the mass of the degraded people, nor could it spring from the line of the priests. For it was then, as with the people so with the priests. They, indeed, as being set apart to witness for Jehovah, were sunk into a debasement greater than that of the ordinary Israelites around them. Nothing can be darker than the figures portrayed for us by the hand of Revelation as constituting the very heart of the priesthood. The high priest's office, and that, as it seems, of the judge of Israel, was now in the hands of Eli, of the house of Ithamar. How it had travelled to that branch of Aaron's family is nowhere distinctly stated, though there is a shadowy revelation of the youth of Eli as having been marked by martial prowess, which, it seems probable, had secured for him the judge's office. In it he had grown old and feeble. God's honour was really dear to the heart of the ancient man; and the loss of the ark of the covenant broke down his spirit as not even the destruction of his two sons could do. But his rule was lax and feeble; feeblest and most lax where, above all others, it should have been strong—over his own sons, who bore the priestly office, and shared the trust and duties of his judgeship. Utter godless worldliness in its two terrible outbreaks of grasping avaricious oppression and flagitious all-sacrificing lust, defaced in them the priestly character; whilst a superstitious valuing of the mere externals of their covenanted service alone lingered on amongst them, witnessing, by its dark presence, against those who had put out the light which once those outward instruments were the divinely fashioned channels to convey to Israel.

To purge out such evils judgment must begin at the house of God. Nor would one act of judgment, however terrible, suffice. The violent death of the high priest, the fall of his two sons in battle, the desecration of Shiloh, and the captivity of the ark—these startling judgments would help perhaps to stir the sleeping heart of Israel. But beyond these the deep degradation of the priesthood had made it needful that the new office of the prophet should stand beside the priest as well as beside the king. The dim outlines of such an approaching dispensation may be traced in the coming of the man of God to Eli with that fearful denunciation whose burning letters of fire have witnessed now in

God's volume for nearly four thousand years to His separated ministers in every age of what must be the end of using for themselves the mighty trust for others committed by the Lord's election to the keeping of His priests (1 Sam. ii. 27—36). But it was in Samuel first that this new ministry was embodied, and the great features of his life are the history of its fulfilment. We see the outlines of the great office beginning to fashion themselves forth even at that tender age when distinct self-consciousness first reveals itself tremblingly within him. The child Samuel—ministering in his linen ephod, clothed with the long garment of honourable proportions which his saintly mother brought him year by year when with his Levitical father she journeyed from Ramah to offer the appointed sacrifice—comes forth first before us from that shrouding which ever hangs so thick around a holy childhood as supernaturally called by God to this prophetic office. How that "uncovering of the ear" was wrought we are not distinctly told; but the whole narrative forbids the supposition that it was upon the mind alone of Samuel that the voice of the Almighty fell. Into all the mystery of that secret visitation which in the dim shadowy light of the sacred precincts, through which the rays of the seven-branched lamp scarcely struggled, we may not safely gaze, but the words "the Lord came, and stood, and called" (1 Sam. iii. 10) must not be weakened or explained away. There was, it is plain, an act upon the part of God antecedent to the impression made on Samuel; and the voice which spoke was doubtless real, as through the still silence of the holy tent its mysterious accents fell upon his watching ear, and syllabled out to his trembling soul the singleness of his own name.

So the long silence of God to His people was broken. That Word of God which was so "precious" from its rarity began again to sound in Israel, and the "open vision" which the mists of idol-worship had veiled revealed to the holy child its sacred proportions. At once the special character of the new office is declared by the prophetic youth being sent to the high priest himself with the message of the Lord.

Those young lips utter the tremendous doom, declaring by the natural feebleness of the instrument how entirely it is the voice of another which speaks through them; and so the old man receives the words. To him plainly they are not Samuel's; his dim eyes can trace "the Presence" being now restored to Israel, and his saddened utterance is that of one who felt through all his frame Jehovah's nearness when he said, "It is the Lord; let Him do what seemeth Him good" (1 Sam. iii. 18). How does the startling sight of the lad of twelve years old (for so his age has been reckoned), standing with such a word of prophecy before the marvelling chief priest, point on to Him, the one true Prophet, in whom all the lines of God's dealings with man converge, of whose days "all the prophets from Samuel, and those that follow after, have foretold," as He too, coming forth from His holy home at Nazareth, was found at twelve years old sitting in the Temple in the midst of the astonished doctors of the law, both hearing them and asking them questions!

When next the prophetic power rested upon

Samuel we know not; but that it did again and again reveal itself is most distinctly stated in the words, "Samuel grew, and the Lord was with him, and did let none of his words fall to the ground. And all Israel, from Dan even to Beersheba, knew that Samuel was established to be a prophet of the Lord. And the Lord appeared again in Shiloh: for the Lord revealed Himself to Samuel in Shiloh by the word of the Lord" (1 Sam. iii. 19—21).

Such had been his childhood and his youth, when the storm of predicted judgment fell upon his people. Roused at last to resistance by intolerable oppression, Israel went out to battle against the Philistines. But though "the word of Samuel came to all Israel," it is not written that they took any counsel of the Lord through him. Their insurrection was but the natural outbreak of the oppressed against the oppressor. There had been no putting away of their idols, no turning to their fathers' God, no seeking, as it seems, of His direction; and so, when "they joined battle Israel was smitten before the Philistines." Then came another exhibition of that spiritual blindness with which the evil lives of their priests had done so much to darken their souls. They had seen abominable iniquity so ostentatiously united with the performance of all the outward acts of their enjoined worship, so abundant around the very doors of the tabernacle (1 Sam. ii. 22) itself, that they had grown to trust in the visible tokens of the invisible presence, instead of believing in the Lord their God. "Let us fetch," was the cry of this dark superstition, "the ark of the covenant of the Lord out of Shiloh unto us, that when it cometh among us, IT may save us out of the hand of our enemies." This was a form of misbelief into which the dark hosts of infidel Philistia could enter, and they too trembled at the coming of the ark. But they trembled needlessly. Israel must be taught its lesson by the hands of the heathen. The people of Jehovah must know that not in the priesthood, or in sacrifice, or in the shrine of Shiloh, or in the ark itself, but in the living God was their defence against their enemies; and so, as before, "Israel was smitten, and there was a very great slaughter, and the ark of God was taken, and the two sons of Eli, Hophni and Phinehas, were slain." Then was Ichabod indeed written on Shiloh, and upon every door-post in Israel. Then indeed did Philistia triumph. For twenty years, as it seems, from this decisive victory she held her cruel heathen sway over the people of Jehovah.

Where Samuel was during this interval, we know not. It was doubtless needful for him to be thus for a season withdrawn from action and observation. His holy childhood and his prophetic youth needed calm, silence, introspection, and secret communion with God, to mature the great strength of his after life. Like St. Paul in Arabia, like a greater than St. Paul at Nazareth after that communing in the temple, he was hidden away by God; hidden, it would seem, like the son of Mary when He left Jerusalem with her for almost twenty years before He was manifested to Israel.

Those twenty years of Samuel's hidden life were a weary time for Israel. Throughout their span Philistia asserted and cemented her dominion over the chosen people. This was probably the season of Samson's single-handed acts of heroic bravery, ending with his mighty destruction of his enemies under the crashing ruins of the Dagon house at Gaza. Samson's deeds of heroism must have stirred many hearts in Israel and aroused the sunken spirits of her sons. But they needed a deeper awakening yet before they could break the yoke of the heathen. There must be a turning of their hearts to God before He would bare His arm for their deliverance. For such a return to Him the sorrows of these twenty years had been preparing their souls. The ark abode in Kirjath Jearim. The time was long; for it was twenty years, and all the house of Israel lamented after the Lord. For such a time the prophet had been kept in that still shelter of the hand of the Almighty. Now he suddenly appears again in Israel. His words catch the tone of that lamenting penitence which had at last begun to stir the national heart. "If ye do return unto the Lord with all your hearts, then put away the strange gods and Ashtaroth from among you, and prepare your hearts unto the Lord and serve Him only, and He will deliver you out of the hand of the

Philistines." And they answered to his call, and put away the strange gods. And He gathered them at Mizpeh for a searching national humiliation. Then in the absence of the ark, and with Shiloh desolate, and the great priestly office in abeyance, the Prophet, under the leading of the Spirit, himself offered a burnt-offering, and made intercession for his people; and God accepted them. To the wild, passionate Samson it had been given "*to begin* to deliver Israel out of the hands of the Philistines." But the strong man had lacked that turning of the heart to God with which the new Nazarite opened his commission. He was to effect what the other had begun; to him was given the far greater charge of beating down Philistia, and at once he set about fulfilling it. Even as he offered the sacrifice the fierce cry of a coming multitude mingled wildly with his prayer; the weeping penitents looked up to see the great Prophet in the long mantle, which from his holy childhood had ever been his garb, standing with his long Nazarite locks floating on the hill-side breeze, in the energy of supplication; "crying unto the Lord" before the altar of burnt-offering, whilst on the other side they could already note the dark hosts of Philistia marching on with all the confidence bred by accustomed victory to the dreaded encounter. Then in his prophetic power Samuel poured down upon the astonished assailants the ancient might of Israel, when loud above all the din of the battle broke forth on every side of heaven the pealing answer of Jehovah's thunder. A panic terror fell upon the uncircumcised, and they were utterly discomfited, and slain with such a slaughter that they were "subdued and came no more unto the coast of Israel; and the hand of the Lord was against the Philistine all the days of Samuel."

The wearied land rested and breathed again with ease under the great deliverance. The cities which the Philistines had taken from Israel were delivered out of the hands of the heathen; the neighbouring Amorite tribes made peace with the conquerors, and "Samuel judged Israel all the days of his life. He went from year to year in circuit to Bethel, and Gilgal, and Mizpeh, and judged Israel in all those places, and his return was to Ramah, for there was his house, and there he judged Israel, and there he built an altar unto the Lord." Such he was in his official life as judge over Israel; of an incorruptible purity, of unwearied diligence, of undisputed power, of life-long continuance.

But there was another side to this great character. In him the temporal administration of the judge, noble as it was, is cast wholly into the shade by the brightness of his prophetic office. This was, as we have seen, a new administration of the One Spirit. So new was it that St. Peter dates from Samuel the rise of the prophetic utterances which announced the coming of Messiah's kingdom of grace. "Yea, and all the prophets, from Samuel and those that follow after, have likewise foretold of these days" (Acts iii. 24).

This novelty of the office would of itself make its first administration as a new development of the working of the Spirit of God a matter of the deepest interest. But beside this, two circumstances of the life of Samuel tend to aggravate its grandeur and bring out all its variety of aspect. The first was, that for him it was appointed to guide the difficult transition of Israel's political organization from a divinely ruled republic into a regularly constituted monarchy. He was the last of the judges, and under his rule their long line, which through four hundred and fifty years had been God's gift to His people, passed into that of the anointed kings of Israel.

The second cause of the greatness of Samuel's prophetic administration is to be found in the character of Saul, by whom he stood as an external conscience; as a director, and revealer, and speaker of the Will of God to one of the most wayward of men. It was not without a struggle of his human will and a shock to his natural affections that Samuel heard the first cry of the people for a king. There was in it ingratitude to him; there was rebellion against the order of deliverers which God had already given them; there was an earthly craving to be like unto the nations round about them. "The thing displeased Samuel;" but his refuge was near, and he "prayed unto the Lord." "Hearken," was the answer, "unto their voice, for they have not rejected thee, but they have rejected me." Their sin was an impatient forestalling of what it was the Will of God that they should have in His way and at His time. How grandly does the great prophet's form stand out when seen against the background of the restless people's earthly clamouring! In him all natural indignation dies out at once. The Voice has spoken to him, and it is enough. His faith accepts without the shadow of a struggle what he now knows to be "the Will of God." At once he proceeds to prepare the chosen of the Lord for his vocation, and then to anoint him king, and to secure to him the undivided following of the people. Hero-like, he is free from every taint of jealousy. He exalts to the uttermost the new monarch. "See ye," he says to all the people, "him whom the Lord hath chosen, that there is none like him among all the people" (1 Sam. x. 24); and the people, catching the enthusiasm from him, "shouted and said, God save the King."

All the attributes of the young king tended to kindle such a passion of loyalty. Commanding in stature, eminent in personal beauty, brave and successful when first tried on the field of battle, his bearing was ennobled by a most gracious and winning modesty. Doubtless the prophet's eye looked on to a reign of holy obedience to Jehovah's Will; to the earthly monarchy being indeed the true reflection upon earth of the heavenly King; to the consolidation of the tribes of Israel; to the subjugation of all their enemies; to their establishment, as a true world-kingdom amongst the nations of the earth, bearing Jehovah's name and upheld by His might. But, alas! beneath those flowery meadows and graceful uplands there were already struggling volcanic fires which wanted opportunity alone to burst forth with destructive vehemence. The real temper of the young monarch was too soon shown. The relation between the king and the prophet, as it was established by God, was, that prophetic utterances were to be received by the ruler of His people as coming directly from His own mouth. Early in Saul's reign his obedience to such "a word" was tried with some severity. In the third year of his reign his gallant son

Jonathan smote the garrison of the Philistines on the hill of Geba. Forthwith the whole might of their old oppressors was put forth for one great effort, to reimpose upon their escaping victims the detested yoke of the uncircumcised.

The Philistines gathered themselves together to fight with Israel, thirty thousand chariots and six thousand horsemen, "a people as the sand that is on the sea-shore in multitude." The scarcely recovered courage of the men of Israel fainted at the sight. The greater number hid themselves away from the terrible enemy "in caves, and in thickets, and in rocks, and in high places, and in pits;" even the few less faint-hearted men who still kept the field "followed Saul trembling." It seemed to the eye of sense that there was madness in waiting, as the prophet had bid him do, seven days in Gilgal, until he came down and offered sacrifice, and showed him what he should do (1 Sam. x. 8). That waiting appeared simply ruinous. Day by day the enemy grew bolder; day by day his own troops more down-hearted and demoralised. The winds of danger told sorely upon the ill-cemented mass, and like the sands under the blast of the desert, they were scattered from him.

Still for seven days he waited, fretting under the command, and with a growing impatience at its unreasonable requirement. The seventh day came, and the prophet still tarried; longer the rising wilfulness of the king's nature could not submit, and disobediently he himself offered the sacrifice. His disobedience was his sin. The ark of God was not in its place: the prophetic commission superseded the priestly. Samuel himself offered not as a priest, which he was not, but as a prophet. The king's sin was not an intrusion of himself into the priestly office, it was a simple sin of wilful disobedience, under strong temptation, to the word of Jehovah, spoken by the mouth of His prophet. No sooner has he offered than Samuel appears. Saul goes out to seek the prophet's blessing; but that blessing is turned into reproofs, which the excuses of the wayward king cannot turn aside—"Thou hast done foolishly: thou hast not kept the commandment of the Lord thy God. Thy kingdom shall not continue: the Lord hath sought him a man after his own heart, and commanded him to be captain over His people, because thou hast not kept that which the Lord commanded thee" (1 Sam. xiii. 14). Here is the first voice of the thunder of coming judgment; distant, undefined, as from an almost unclouded sky; capable of being averted. It leads to no separation between him and the prophet. Samuel goes up to Gibeah of Benjamin with the king. The Spirit of God has been grieved, but it does not leave him. He strengthens himself on his throne. Years pass on, and bring with them victories and power. "He took the kingdom over Israel, and fought against all his enemies on every side, and whithersoever he turned he vexed them." Once or twice the wilful temper of his soul breaks forth; but on the whole he fights bravely the battle of Israel, and prospers in his ways.

Fourteen years have passed away, when again the discipline of his life gathers itself up into a special trial. The great prophet's voice brings him a new commission from his God, and preludes it by a note of very special warning. "The Lord sent me to anoint thee to be king over his people; now therefore hearken thou unto the voice of the Lord." That tone of adjuration surely tells all. It speaks the prophet's judgment of his character; it tells of prayers and intercession, of days of watching and nights of grief, for one he loved so well, as he saw growing on that darkening countenance the deepening lines of wilfulness. The prophet sees that this will be a crisis in that life-history, with which, by God's own hand, his own has been so strangely intertwined. He gives the king the charge of God to "smite Amalek, to destroy them utterly, and spare none." To go forth on this campaign suited well the martial and violent temper of Saul, and he readily obeyed. The assault was perfectly successful. But the wilful heart of the conqueror could not obey entirely. He could not resist the temptation to bring back in triumph the captive king of Amalek, or to spare the flocks and herds which might enrich Israel. The sentence of God was not long delayed. As he returned with his victorious troops, the prophet met him. That sorrow-stricken countenance, around which hung the long Nazarite locks, now whitened by the snows of ninety years, pale and worn with the long night's unbroken, but ungranted, intercession, as in grief for the offender he had cried unto the Lord all night, might have told all. But he was bidden to speak it out, and so he meets the king in the triumph of his return with a reproof, sterner far than when fourteen years before he had chidden his early disobedience. Now the thunder-cloud, then distant and well-nigh undiscernible, darkens the whole sky, and peals over the sinner's head. "Stay," is the sad and terrible voice as it breaks through the cobweb films of self-deception and excuse, " and I will tell THEE what the Lord hath said to me this night. . . . . The Lord sent thee . . . . and said, Go and utterly destroy the sinners the Amalekites. Wherefore then didst thou not obey the voice of the Lord, but didst fly upon the spoil?" Then comes again, with trembling dishonesty, out of that once strong man's mouth, the poor excuse, " The people . . . . took of the spoil to sacrifice unto the Lord thy God in Gilgal"—the very utterance of dark superstition and mean equivocation. And forthwith, like the darting down of the brightness of the lightning's flash, the prophet's voice gathers itself up into one of those magnificent utterances which, belonging to another and a later dispensation, antedate the coming revelation, and are evidently launched forth from the open "ark of the testimony" of the Highest—"Hath the Lord as great delight in burnt-offerings and in sacrifices as in obeying the voice of the Lord? Behold, to obey is better than sacrifice, and to hearken than the fat of rams. Because THOU hast rejected the word of the Lord, He hath also rejected THEE from being king." And now judgment—as is its terrible wont —gathered round him in contracting circles. The doom was irreversible. "The Strength of Israel is not a man . . . that He should repent."

It was a fearful meeting—it was followed by an almost life-long parting. "Samuel came no more to see Saul until the day of his death." Once only in life, some seventeen years later, the king, when too far hardened in his wilfulness for instruction or reproof, saw again that face, to sink at Naioth under its prophetic power. But still upon the hill of Ramah, where the prophet dwelt, the cry of mourning intercession ceased not: "Nevertheless Samuel mourned for Saul." The judgments of the God that heareth prayer seem to have been stayed by that mighty supplication of him who is classed by the Word of God with Moses, as the greatest of human intercessors. And so, with faithful love, the prophet cried unto his God, until the voice which in his childhood had spoken to him the transference of the priesthood of Eli, now told him of the removal of God's anointing from Saul to David in these fearful tones: "How long wilt thou mourn for Saul, seeing I have rejected him from reigning over Israel? Fill thine horn with oil, and go unto Jesse the Bethlehemite, for I have provided me a king among his sons."

At the peril of his life from the anger of the king, Samuel goes, and guided against his natural judgment to David, pours on his head the anointing oil, and the Spirit of the Lord owns the commanded act, and comes from that day forward upon David. Then the cloud settles darker and darker upon the rejected king. The Spirit of the Lord had departed from him, and an evil spirit from the Lord troubled him. That self-willed heart was haunted by the gloomy delusions which usher in despair. Reason trembled on her seat of rule; whilst passion and hatred led madness on, and seated her instead upon the throne of inward mastery. For years the awful conflict lasted; gleams of light there were, but evermore the darkness deepened, and its evil, half-discerned figures thronged him in wilder and multiplied companionship, and gathered closer around him. Upon David, his preferred successor, all the hatred of his soul concentrated its venom. How must the ever-during "mourning" of the prophet have grown sadder in its tones as he saw the utter wreck of that early brightened life! Happy was it for him that he lived not to see its bitter end upon the mountains of Gilboa. But he had set for all time the great example of the office of the prophet of the Lord, when called to stand in God's name not only by the side of His willing and obedient servant, but also amidst the deep shadows which settled on the wilful king.

Nor was it only the lineaments of this great

model and example which this first of the prophets left for after times. With that prescient eye which belonged to one employed to conduct the nation and the Church of Israel through a great transition in its history, he foresaw the need of providing a new system of training for those who should be his successors in the prophetic office. For this end he formed into fixed societies the sharers of the mysterious gift, which was plainly capable of cultivation and enlargement.

As at every leading crisis of the dealings of God with man, unusual operations of the Spirit marked the time of Samuel. They were not confined to him, though his is far the most conspicuous figure on the canvas. "There was the company of the prophets, and Samuel standing as appointed over them" (1 Sam. xix. 20). These companies of the prophets eminently foreshadow that Church which the greater than Samuel should form. In it, as amongst them, the gift is diffused throughout the whole body; is capable of increase; breaks out in one and in another in separate manifestations, but is still the working of the One Spirit; abounds when sought by all as one, and by each as a part of the whole, but dies out in separation, and languishes in each who is becoming estranged from the common body. Therefore were they gathered by the great Seer, from his insight into the future, into these communions. From these came the spiritual successions which gave Gad and Nathan and Samuel's own grandson Heman to the Church of Israel.

Thus he provided for the time when he no longer could uphold in person the new institution. For he too was bowed by age and must sleep with his fathers. Peacefully and gradually the change passed over him. It was the due end of his even and consistent life. It was a grand parting between him and Israel when he laid down the active exercise of the judge's office to hand it over to the king they had desired. Equable progression from the beginning to the end was the special characteristic of the life of Samuel. No sudden development of military prowess lifted him from common life into the judge's office. The Nazarite vow was marked on him by promise even before he was born; the morning dew of grace glistened on him from his birth; his childhood was open to special visitations of God's grace in the stillness of the sanctuary and amidst the sanctities of Shiloh. Of the life which followed this he could speak without contradiction or dispute: "I am old and grey-headed .... and I have walked before you from my childhood to this day. Behold, here I am, witness against me before the Lord, and before His anointed." The death was like the life; it was the gathering up of the feet into the bed, the calmest lying down to die; the whole inspired record of it is the three solemn words, "And Samuel died." So giveth He His beloved rest. He was buried in his own house at Ramah: there he was born; thither probably he withdrew at the desecration of Shiloh; thence he judged Israel; there he lay down and died. Around him were the lamentations of his people. It is written with expressness of emphasis, "ALL the Israelites were gathered together, and lamented him and buried him." All had known him,—the tall figure, mantle-clad, the long white locks, the reverend countenance—they should see them no more;

no more hear that voice of wise counsel and of brave rebuke. Another mighty one had passed away; one who, like Moses and Joshua, had inaugurated a new dispensation; he, too, was gone —the great prophet, the gifted seer, the upright judge, the inspired hero, he had passed away: the very heart of the nation sighed out its loving, weeping requiem. All Israel, with a mighty lamentation, mourned for Samuel.

Who amongst them all mourned as that son of Jesse on whose head he had, at God's command, poured the anointing oil? Heavy thoughts were in that mighty heart when David passed again from under the shadow of Samuel's dwelling-place at Ramah into the cold bare world which had no resting-place for him, as he "arose and went down to the wilderness of Paran." Doubtless in its waste places he heard again, in loving memory, the echoes of the prevailing "cry" of him who was so great amongst those who "called upon the name of the Lord." Doubtless his own discipline was perfected in this new sorrow, and he learned in losing Samuel to lean more simply and alone on Samuel's God.

DAVID THE KING.

AMONGST all the noble creations of Greek poetry there is no single figure more vividly portrayed than is that of Saul the son of Kish, as he stands before us in the inspired records of Israel.

Every line of his character is as fresh as if he lived yesterday; there is the grand hero-like beauty of his early manhood, the lofty stature, the strong arm, the unflinching nerves, the quick eagle-eye of the successful general, the generosity to unworthy opponents, which makes success so graceful and imperial command so easy to endure.

To this bright morning succeeds the overclouded noonday; the mists gather earliest and thickest round these heights of unexpected royal elevation to which the Benjamite commoner was raised. Through the ingenuous evenness of his youthful countenance, the strong lines of growing self-will begin to break with volcanic violence. Year by year they develop and they darken, until they fix themselves in an aspect of habitual gloom. The green valley, the wavy corn-field, the sunlit stream are left behind us; we are in the gorges of the mountains, and its hard rocks frown morosely on us.

Still for a season the clouds open, and rays of light dart down which for the moment make these wild fastnesses seem glad. But these soon pass away. The clouds lower and thicken and blacken. The night, with its terrors, comes before its time; in its darkness the storm which has so long been gathering breaks with a sudden crash; and we gaze with breathless awe upon its fury.

From that day of evil omen, when, the last word of warning spoken, Samuel turned away from the self-willed king, to come no more to see him to the day of his death (1 Sam. xv. 35); that darkness began to settle down upon him. The "evil spirit from God," with fewer intermissions, and with a wilder vehemence, stirred his darkening soul to phrensy. The madness which was latent in his constitution openly declared itself, and its thick shadow was by degrees drawn like a darkening pall over his life. Deeds of violence multiplied in his hands. The blood-thirsty hatred which madly alternated with a parental love for the son of Jesse, the charmer away of his own gloom, increased upon him with the violence of convulsive spasms. At one moment he saw before him his "son David," and "loved him greatly" (xvi. 21: xxiv. 16): at the next moment the deliverer of his people could but see in him the abhorred successor to his throne, whom, in his jealousy and fury, he would pin with his lance to the wall. Then came the cruel slaughter of the priests of God, with all their families; and the murder of the Gibeonites, to whom the faith of Israel had been plighted. Over this life of violence the heavens above him blackened; around it the keen-sighted vultures gathered. God answered him no more. The terrible silence which precedes the lightning's flash had fallen on him. He groans out his agony in the despairing cry, "God is departed from me, and answereth me no more, neither by prophets nor by dreams." As God departed, his enemies multiplied in increasing swarms around him. Again the Philistines came up and filled the land; the tide of invasion swept over the plain of Esdraelon up to the hills of Shunem Higher up the range, clinging to their mountain ramparts, were encamped the trembling hosts of Israel. At such a moment that blank dead silence of the spirit-world around him became too terrible for the endurance of the dark-souled king; and rather than bear longer its stifling horror, he went to one of the tribe of necromancers whom his own severe rule had wellnigh terminated. There, in the gloomy cavern of Endor, the Evil One was suffered, in the likeness of the dead prophet of his youth, to chant back to him the despairing utterances of his dark soul. The hollow voice of the fiend claimed his own. "To-morrow shalt thou and thy sons be with me." Then died out the spirit of the wretched man, and his giant form fell prostrate on the earth. To raise him up, to force him to take the food he needed, was his servants' work. But to them it was not given to soothe the convulsive struggles of that broken heart.

The morrow came; the hosts of the Philistines swept up the mountain's side; the great captain's heart was already dead; his old skill in arms had departed from him, and the heathen triumphed. "The men of Israel fled before the Philistines, and fell down slain in Mount Gilboa; and the Philistines followed hard upon Saul and upon his sons: and the battle went sore against Saul, and the archers hit him, and he was sore wounded of the archers." Then came the black ending of that life, once of such brilliant promise, since of such varied incident. He falls upon his sword, and, still lingering on in the death-anguish, is slain at his own desire by the young man, the Amalekite, who hastens to Ziklag with the royal crown and bracelet, to gain from David the gifts and the promotions for which his greedy soul longed; but which turned for him into the stern sentence, "How wast thou not afraid to stretch out thy hand against the Lord's anointed? Thy blood be upon thy head. Go near, and fall upon him" (2 Sam. i. 14, 15). At so dark a time for Israel the long-promised crown passed to David. Protracted in its duration, and most various in its features, had been the discipline by which he had been trained, not for this succession only; but for the higher dignity of being the prophet-king who should above all others be the type of Him who should deliver not Israel only, but humanity from its enemies, and who should sit for ever on the throne of David.

For it was needed for this higher office that the character of David should gather into itself—so far as might be—all the various workings of the heart of man. This is the special attribute of the life and character of the royal son of Jesse. It was thoroughly and intensely human. In this lies the first great contrast between him and his predecessor. There is a hard, narrow separateness of soul marked in every line of the character of Saul; he is a wayward, wilful, self-determined man, well-nigh incapable of any real sympathy with others; parted almost as widely from his loving son Jonathan as he is from David, whom he hates as a rival. Such an one could learn little of the workings of that human heart which is so immeasurable in the multitude and compass of its tones. Deep as were his sorrows; he never knew the grace of contrition. Thus, his dark heart is full of sullenness and suspicion, inviting the entrance of the Evil One, who came at his bidding, and closed with yet sterner bars all the avenues to his soul. In every one of these particulars David is the most complete contrast to Saul. Whose soul does not answer, as the image in the glass to the countenance bent upon it, to every one of his Psalms? How endless in their variety, how vast in their compass are the notes drawn out of that most human soul by the breath of the Spirit of God! In our seasons of joy how naturally does our praise and thanksgiving break forth in the words of his songs of gladsomeness! In times of terror how do we fly with him to the strong fortress of the name of his God! In our bitter anguish, in what other words can we pour forth our woe as we can in his? In that saddest of all hours, when the sense of sin presses us into the very mire, where can we find such words of heart-broken confession as in the 51st of his Psalms? More by far than any other saint in the Old Testament does he stand out before us as the type of Him " who hath suffered being tried, that He might know how to succour them that are tried."

The second most distinctly marked point of contrast between the two characters is this: the one ever drew nigh to God, the just, the righteous, the almighty, the all-living God, in whom he lived and moved and had his being; the other, with all his better impulses and occasional illapses even of the spirit of prophecy, never knew God. A dark, unloving, superstitious fear, which bred neither humiliation, nor trust, nor true obedience, filled the one heart; a loving, trusting, delight in God, the true parent of humility, self-distrust, and obedience, possessed the other. The two different natures utter repeatedly the deep secret of the diversity of their inner being. Thus, when Saul had broken the commandment of God, delivered to him by Samuel, the slavishness of his religion comes out in the words, "I said the Philistines will come down now upon me to Gilgal: and I have not entreated the face of the Lord. I forced myself therefore and offered a burnt-offering." Here again the lack of all true contrition breaks forth in the utterance, "I have sinned: yet honour me now, I pray thee, before the elders of my people." In what sharp contrast with these stand the parallel utterances of David's heart after his great sin! "Thou desirest not sacrifice; else would I give it: thou delightest not in burnt-offering. The sacrifices of God are a broken spirit: a broken and a contrite heart, O God, Thou wilt not despise" (Psalm li. 16, 17). And again, instead of thinking of the judgment of the "elders of his people," what a vision is given us of the undivided singleness with which his eye looks straight up to God in those marvellous words which have ever since set the tone of every penitent's return to God!—"Against Thee, Thee only have I sinned, and done this evil in Thy sight. I acknowledge my transgression, and my sin is ever before me. Wash me throughly from my iniquity, and cleanse me from my sin" (Psalm li. 2—4). This was the central point of that character which made him the man after God's own heart. Here again the great image of the One Only Man who was ever perfectly after the heart of God, is prefigured in his progenitor after the flesh. In the outlines, blurred in David by sin, we can see, as in some broken mirror, the image of one who came not to do His own will, but the will of Him that sent Him.

The history of David's life is the record of his education in this high grace by the hand of God It began in his earliest years. Separated by disparity of years from his seven brothers, whilst they lived in the world, he, according to the simple use of that early age, kept his father's sheep, upon the hill pastures near to Bethlehem. There, doubtless, the angels of God met him; they who, in after time, revealed to shepherds—like himself abiding upon those grassy uplands of Bethlehem, keeping watch over their flocks by night—the good tidings of great joy, that in the city of David was born a Saviour which is Christ the Lord. They bent their gaze upon this chosen youth, fair even to their eyes,—"ruddy, and withal of a beautiful countenance, and goodly to look on," as he wandered apart from men with his flock, communing with nature, drinking in the soft dews of prophetic inspiration, and breathing out the holy utterance of his untainted heart unto the God of Israel. Little did he dream of the future for which he was preparing. He had no desire to change that favoured portion for any other. God had set him there to keep those sheep in the wilderness. For God he kept them; with God he communed as he changed their pasture, beat off the lion and the bear, and led them to the water's side. His own charge drew up his thoughts to the Almighty One, who deigned to be his shepherd, who kept him from want, who made him to lie down in these green pastures, who led him beside the still waters, who made him fear no evil, because the Mightiest was with him, even though he walked through the valley of the shadow of death (Psalm xxiii.). Nor was there anything dreamy or enervating in his shepherd's life. Its solitariness braced up his spirit, and its dangers formed within him the habit of ready action based on simple trust in his God. When the lion and the bear came forth against his wilderness flock, and took a lamb for which he was accountable out of the fold, he went out after him and caught him by his beard, and smote him, and slew him. It was to him but a natural act; he knew that he did it not in his own might, but in the strength of that Lord who "delivered him out of the paw of the lion and out of the paw of the bear;" and in that presence the accidents of great and small, and the outside terrors before which his natural spirit would have quailed, vanished like the wreath of mist in the brightness of the sunshine.

So was his faith nurtured. Then there brake in upon it that sudden transition with which the East has ever been familiar, which carried him direct into the court of Saul. The moody madness of the wilful king had already increased upon him into fits which made his courtiers counsel him to seek the soothing of his troubled spirit by the calming influence of minstrelsy He consents; and David is brought before him

He stands before the king, "cunning in playing, mighty and valiant, prudent in matters, a comely person, and one with whom the Lord is:" and when the fit falls upon the king, David takes his harp, and plays with his hand, and the distraught soul owns his power. Saul was refreshed, and was well, and the evil spirit departed from him. Then the inspired minstrel leaves the melancholy court, and wanders again, rejoicing in his recovered liberty, upon the mountainside, waking its echoes by the song of praise which he so well loved.

But this is not to last. War breaks out with the Philistines. The elder sons of Jesse follow Saul in the camp. To them the youngest is sent down by their old father, to carry them supplies, and to learn their estate. His journey was so ordered by his God that it brought him to the tent just as all Israel was trembling before the threatenings of the giant of Gath.

In those early wars the issues of the greatest battles, which were but a series of personal conflicts, turned often on the single strength and prowess of such a champion. For days the mail-clad giant insulted with his threatening taunts the hosts and God of Israel. The king offered noble rewards to any who would meet and overcome him in battle. But of all the chosen warriors of Israel not one was found to venture on the unequal fray; and so the champion of the uncircumcised waxed daily bolder in his insults and his boasts. As David passes through the hosts, he hears the whispers of the trembling soldiery, and at last sees the Philistine giant as he stalks forth on his march of defiance. The heart of the young hero shudders as he hears those words of blasphemy The trusting heart of God's servant could see no ground for fearing one who came forth to defy Jehovah. And he, with the naturalness of his character, at once speaks out his thoughts; and in the same simple energy of courage with which he had risen against the lion and the bear, he is ready to go forth against the champion of the uncircumcised. The rumour that one was found ready to take up the challenge is soon brought to Saul. He sends at once for the daring warrior, and finds, when he is ushered into his presence, that it is the minstrel youth whose harp erewhile had brought him rest. It was a strange interview; the warrior-king, himself well-nigh of giant stature, could not stand before the Philistine; and what in such an encounter could this young stripling do? To the self-confident man of this world, David's simple faith was well-nigh inconceivable; and the ever-ready discouragement of the voice of the flesh rises unbidden to those wilful lips. "Thou art not able to go against this Philistine." And when convinced, it may be by David's bearing, that the Highest had indeed inspired the venture still the king would encompass him in armour before he trusts the mighty issue to his hands. David tries and rejects the armour. "I cannot go in these:"—and strong only in Jehovah's might he goes forth, with nothing save his shepherd's equipment, against the champion of Philistia. Then the mighty arm of flesh is beaten down by unseen hands before Jehovah's servant, and David is brought back again to court, no longer as the mere minister to Saul's necessity, as one whose sweet minstrelsy can charm to rest the troubled soul, and drive away the evil spirit, but to be "set over the men of war." Still the contrast between these two men holds consistently out to the end. "This day," says David to the uncircumcised champion, "this day will the Lord deliver thee into mine hand .... for the battle is the Lord's, and He will give you into our hands." In God, from first to last, is all his confidence. Saul, on the other hand, true to his original discouragement of the boldness bred by the divine afflatus falling on the hero heart—true to his seeking, when he doubtfully committed to David's hand the championship of Israel, to secure the defence of the royal armour for the stripling—enquires eagerly of Abner, the captain of the host, whose son is this youth; not from any want of recognition of David, but to ascertain whether his coming of any warrior lineage may justify some hope of a prosperous issue of the unequal conflict.

This mighty act of daring, for which a daily walk of faith in lesser instances had been preparing him, was the turning-point in David's life. He was now "set over the men of war;" he "was accepted in the sight of all the people;" the hand which had led him to the mountain sheepfolds now beckoned him on to the forefront of the nation.

Here is a new stage reached in his life's discipline. The affections of the king's son are set upon him, and his courtly life is brightened by the sunshine of that pure, disinterested love which has embalmed for all time the name of Jonathan. Need enough had he of such solace in the life he had to lead in that troubled court. The bitter jealousy of Saul's nature soon woke up against him, with all that intensity of hate which only jealousy can breed. Whether he had heard of that anointing by Samuel at Bethlehem, which must have brought back to him, with an indescribable bitterness of heart, his own anointing in the land of Zuph, we know not. But such knowledge was not needed to wake up this bitter envy. The prophet had distinctly told him in the day of his sin, that the Lord had rent the kingdom from him, and had given it to a neighbour that was better than he. And in David he could read the marks of such a man;

for this young man was not only hymned in the triumphal songs of the daughters of Israel, and beloved by his own son, but accepted in the sight of all the people, and even of his own servants. Saul looked upon him and trembled. How strange was the destiny which had brought this dangerous rival into his presence! What evil might it not work against himself! And so his dark heart began at once to lay schemes for the destruction of his rival. In the paroxysms of his madness this deep-seated hatred led him to seek to slay, with his own hand, the minstrel who was charming him to rest. Such attempts, indeed, at personal violence passed away with the fit of madness which provoked them. But down in that once heroic soul, which sin had sunk into the baseness of cowardice, a yet deeper malignity was forming. "Saul was afraid of David because the Lord was with him, and was departed from Saul" (1 Sam. xviii. 12). This coward hatred of his sunken spirit vented itself first in plots to slay his fancied enemy by the hand of the Philistines, and then in undisguised attempts upon the life which seemed to threaten his sovereignty. By these last David is driven first from the court, and at length from the land of Israel. There gathers round him unbidden a band of outcasts, who, in their wild lawlessness, own the control of his master spirit: and thus is reached yet another stage in his manifold training For now was forced upon him a friendly intercourse with Moab, and some of the tribes of Philistines. Slayer as he was of Goliath, yet as the enemy of Saul, they esteemed him the friend of Philistia, and Achish, the king of Gath, gave him royal shelter, expecting, doubtless, the succour of his heroic band in future conflicts with Israel. So he sojourned amongst the uncircumcised, to be called, like his greater son, in the fulness of time, up out of his Egypt. Meanwhile, this tarrying in Philistia was another instrument of his training, for it nurtured that largeness of sympathy which he needed when he was the king of Israel. Provision for this had already been made in his descent from the Moabitish Ruth, but, in no way, probably, but by thus being forced to tarry with the Moabites and Philistines, could the shepherd of the hill-country of Bethlehem have practically learned the lesson which fitted him for his wider after-mission.

A mighty training, too, lay in that wild outlaw life for the knowledge and government of men. Nothing but the completest personal supremacy could hold such unruly elements under any species of command; and David, the unwilling head of such a following, learned in mastering them the secret of governing men, and knitting together their discordant hearts into an harmonious unity. By little and little that band had swollen in number; whilst names, great in after-history, began to be found in it. The prophet Gad, afterwards "the king's seer," had joined him at the cave of Adullam, and declared to him the oracles of God; shortly after, on the slaughter of the priests by Saul, Abiathar escaped, and "fled to David to Keilah, with the ephod in his hand." Thenceforward the life of Abiathar was intertwined with that of David, and "he was afflicted in all wherein David was afflicted." His brethren, too, and all his father's house, no longer safe from Saul's increasing violence, came down to him. His aged father and his mother he lodged, till he knew what God might do for him, with the king of Moab, upon whose hospitality, through Ruth, his mother, Jesse had hereditary claims. His brothers and his nephews, those hard, doughty sons of Zeruiah, joined his band, and, unshielded by that inward communing with God, which kept amidst such rudenesses the heart of David tender, learned there that familiarity with deeds of violence and blood which stained so deeply their after-lives. Great in that rugged band must have been the power of that passionate tenderness with which the heroic heart of David overflowed. Who can hear, even now over the chasm of three thousand years, the voice of longing, out of the dry and desert cave of Adullam, for the water, which, from the well of Bethlehem, had slaked his young thirst, without understanding how the three worthies came to break through the host of the Philistines to draw the water out of the well for their beloved chief; or without feeling how more than ever they would have loved and followed him, when David "would not drink of it, but poured it out unto the Lord, because it was to him as the blood of these men that have put their lives in jeopardy?" (1 Chron. XI. 17.)

A hard and restless life it was, to be hunted as a partridge on the mountain; so hard that at last it drove the chief into settling reluctantly his band across the borders of Israel, amongst the heathen people. A long waiting it was for the promise. Seven years had completed their tale since the anointing-oil was poured upon his head; and he was still an outlaw.

Still upon his soul was the bitterness of having been "driven out from abiding in the inheritance of the Lord" (1 Sam. xxvi. 19), of being parted from all the covenanted acts of worship, and being bidden to "Go and serve other gods." What an unveiling have we of the bitterness of his soul; what an insight into his secret strength, in that Psalm which he poured out in the dark recesses of the Adullam cave, when, with a spirit overwhelmed with shame, he "cried unto the Lord with his voice: Thou art my refuge, and my portion in the land of the living; attend unto my cry, for I am brought very low; deliver me from my persecutors. Bring my soul out of prison that I may praise Thy name." For a year and four months he had been living in that town of Ziklag, which Achish, the son of Maoch, king of Gath, had given to him. Thither, on one of those many days of sadness, came a man out of the camp from Saul, with his clothes rent and earth upon his head. He came with the news of Israel's overthrow—of the death of Saul, and his beloved Jonathan; and to bear to him, as the designated king, the bracelet and crown of his predecessor. The messenger was an Amalekite, and he boasted to the exiled chief, in all the greedy expectancy with which his heathen heart craved for a royal largess, that his hand had ended the life of the wilful king. But he had misjudged utterly the temper of the son of Jesse. With the same unshaken reverence of devotion to the anointed of the Lord which had prevented him from avenging himself upon his persecutor, which had made his conscience smite him when he had but cut off the fringe of the king's garment, he now repudiates utterly the alleged deed of blood, and sentenced to instant execution the self-confessed murderer of the king; and then there breathed upon him the spirit of prophecy, and in a Psalm of lamentation he wept the end of Saul, and of Jonathan his son.

But other duties were now immediately before him. He enquired of the Lord, and the Lord said, "Go up to Hebron." Thither he repaired. Then came the men of Judah up to Hebron, the holy city of their tribe, where the patriarchs were buried, and anointed him king over the House of Judah.

Years of war followed with the adherents of the old dynasty. But David waxed stronger and stronger, and the House of Saul weaker and weaker, until the time came for fulfilling God's promise to him; and after this disputed reign of seven years and six months, when David was thirty-seven years old, "all the tribes of Israel came to him in Hebron, and anointed him king over Israel, and he reigned thirty and three years over all Israel and Judah."

Then was seen the fruit of all that long and hard discipline by which his royal heart had secretly been trained. In every respect, he was a great king—in war, in administration, in magnificence, in external prosperity. He was not like Saul, the ruler of a set of tribes; the kingdom was established in his hand. He begins by subduing the citadel of Jebus, and constituting Jerusalem, the city of David, a true, national metropolis. He brings up the ark, and sets it in his place. He establishes regulated forms of worship; he gathers together the company of singers, and of those skilled in all instruments of music, to exalt the praises of Jehovah, and from his throne of empire, under the inspiration of the Spirit of his God, he pours forth his sacred lyrics, to be sung by grateful hearts before the ark of the everlasting covenant. We can almost hear the creaking of the gates of the old fortress of Jebus, as their hinges swung sullenly open to admit the ark of the living God; we can almost hear that glad shout of the rejoicing king:—" Lift up your heads, O ye gates, and be ye lift up, ye everlasting doors, and the King of Glory shall come in. . . . Who is this King of Glory? The Lord of Hosts; He is the King of Glory"

All this, moreover, was no formal recognition of the nation's God, but the real pouring forth of David's very heart before Him who had ever been his refuge. How grand is the humility of the noble utterance with which he rebuked the pride of Michal's heart, who, the true laughter of her father, could not bear to see her husband humble himself before her God in the sight of all his people!—"It was before the Lord which chose me. . . . to appoint me ruler over the people of the Lord, over Israel: therefore will I play before the Lord. . . And I will yet be more vile than thus, and will be base in mine own sight" (2 Sam. vi. 21).

In the like temper it was that he longed to build a house for God. As soon as the Lord had given him rest round about from all his enemies, the king said unto Nathan the Prophet, "See, now, I dwell in a house of cedar, but the ark of God dwelleth within curtains." But the great offering was not to be accepted from his hand. His son was to build the house. If there had been anything of self-will in David's purpose, this refusal might have chafed him

But no! he at once accepted the word of God as right, and humbly prepares materials for him at whose hands God would deign to accept the offering. "Who am I," he said, as he poured out his full breast before the Lord, "Who am I, O Lord God, and what is my house, that thou hast brought me hitherto. . . . and what can David say more unto Thee? For THOU, Lord God, knowest Thy servant" (2 Sam. vii. 18—20).

Great indeed must have been the effect upon his people of the king's loving devotion to his God! We may easily conceive what a change it was from the dark shadows cast on every side by the throne of Saul; from the dull torpor of the absent ark, and unvisited tabernacle; from the silence of the voice of praise, and the dumbness of Jehovah's utterance; from the "God has departed from me, and answereth not." He did indeed by psalm, by song, and by example, wake up at once the nation's heart to praise their God. With this burst of internal religious life broke forth the power of Israel against her hereditary enemies. The king himself was "a mighty man, a man of war" (2 Sam. xviii. 8), and round about him were the comrades in arms, who had learned with him, in the experience of his years of exile, all the hard secrets of the camp: "They that be with him are valiant men." These "chief of the mighty men strengthened themselves with him in his kingdom" (1 Chron. xi. 10). Under them the army was now thoroughly organized; so that "David waxed greater and greater, for the Lord was with him." Around him, on every side, sped on the wave of conquest, sweeping over the Philistines, the Moabites, the Syrians, the Edomites, and Ammonites, until the promise of God was fulfilled, and he and Israel had rest from all their enemies round about them.

Within his kingdom, too, his throne was exalted, for "the Lord preserved him wherever he went, and he reigned over all Israel, and executed judgment and justice unto all his people." How calm, bright, and glorious a mid-day of sunshine had that stormy, cloud-canopied morning ushered in at last! Surely, if the story ended here, every eye could see in it the parable and promise of the setting up, through persecution and martyrdom, of the kingdom of the Prince of Peace, the Son of David.

But here ends abruptly the typical resemblance, up to this point so startling in its exactness. One deadly element of future woe mingled itself with the establishment of the kingdom of David. His family was formed and governed on the model of the Eastern kings. Though the monarchs of Israel had been commanded not greatly to multiply wives, yet polygamy had never been absolutely forbidden, and David practised it freely.

Thus, when his throne had been thoroughly established, he brought into his family the curse of the Harem. An utter lack of discipline amongst his children was one of its first-fruits; and it brought yet deeper ill than even that; for it poisoned all the springs of family life and tainted it with ever-recurring impurity: working in him and in all around him its universal fruits of impurity, jealousy, hatred, incest, and blood.

David's own great sin, written with such plainness in the sacred record, opens this dark and dismal chapter of his history. Acts, which in the established Eastern life of the heathendom are too common for any special notice, are written down in the inspired record of the life of one who had known the living God with their own true names in the black entries of the catalogue of crime, as adultery and murder.

There is no more terrible, there is no more instructive portion of the word of God, than this whole record. The long death-sleep of that once living soul; its awakening under the prophet's voice; its deep repentance; its free forgiveness; its long, heavy, repeated, almost incessant chastisement, speak to every ear which is not altogether deaf, lessons of the holiness and truth, of the severity and love, of the justice and mercy of the Lord our God, which is borne perhaps with equal force in no other record of His ways with man. All David's after life is clouded by these chastisements. The sword never more departed from his house. The murder of his guilty first-born, Amnon; the treason of Absalom, and his miserable end; the rebellion of Adonijah, who had inherited all that partial love which had been so largely given to Absalom, his elder brother; and who, like Absalom, was a "very goodly man;" whom his father "had never displeased at any time," even "by saying, Why hast thou done so?" One after another, even to his life's end, these waves of sorrow broke over the mourning king, and woke from that harp, which of old had poured forth with such exuberance its joyful jubilations, the dirges of an almost broken heart. His flight from Absalom sets the full cup of his sadness most visibly before us.

How deeply stirred was that loving spirit when the messenger came to David from Hebron, saying, "The hearts of the men of Israel are after Absalom!" How did the message wake up within him the echo of the old sentence, "The sword shall never depart from thy house!" More, as it seems, to prevent the deeds of blood and crime which he dreads for Absalom than from love of his own life, the king resolves to quit Jerusalem before the troops, headed by their unnatural leader, can approach to assault it. "Let us flee," says that brave old voice, "make speed to depart, lest Absalom overtake us suddenly and bring evil upon us and smite the city with the edge of the sword. So the king went forth and all the people with him." And what a departing it was! The very love and faithfulness of the rest lent a deeper note of tragedy to Absalom's unnatural treason. To Ittai the Gittite, the king says, "Return to thy place .... for thou art a stranger and an exile. Whereas thou camest but yesterday, should I this day make thee go up and down with us?" But the faithful retainer would not quit him against whom his own son conspired. "As the Lord liveth, and as my lord the king liveth," is his answer, "surely in what place my lord the king shall be, whether in death or life, there also shall thy servant be." So he followed the king, and so did all the people, till all the country wept with a loud voice; so passed the king over the brook Kidron, and he went up by the ascent of Olivet, and wept as he went up, and had his head covered, and he went barefoot.

Whose eye cannot see here the almost strange manifestations which break forth in all these old passages of sacred history setting before us the One towards whom they were ever bearing on the race of man, and showing us darkly in a mirror all that was appointed for Him? For did not He too, because He was bearing the sinner's burden, go forth with His faithful followers over that same brook Kidron, which washed His feet as it had done His father David's? Did not the faithful disciples and the weeping women cross it with Him, and with Him climb the ascent of Olivet? and was there not, to set against Ittai's passionate boast of loyalty, the loud promises of Peter? and was there not the treachery of Judas to repeat the wickedness of Absalom? and in the great central figure, too, was there not the uttermost submission to the Will of God, when David sent back into the city the ark of the covenant, in that voice, "If I shall find favour in the eyes of the Lord, He will bring me again, and show me both it and His habitation. But if He thus say, I have no delight in thee, behold, here am I, let Him do to me as seemeth good unto Him?" Are not those words in very deed a prophecy of that true Son's utterance when Peter, Zadok like, rendered uncommanded service, "Put up thy sword into the sheath; the cup which my Father hath given me, shall I not drink it?" And but once again, may we not see in the turning back upon himself to his own destruction of the worldly-wise sagacity of the counsel of Achitophel, a mysterious adumbration of the way in which the spiritual master of all wicked devices brought upon himself the bruising of the head when he sought to wreak his hatred on the woman's seed?

So the great king fled from Absalom—fled only to return with his heart well-nigh broken by the life-long sorrow of his bitter grief for the "young man" who had been cut unrepentant down in the midst of his accumulated crimes of actual treason and meditated parricide.

Never, it would seem, during the eight years which his life yet lasted was this heavy shadow removed from his soul; for amongst his "last words" he breatnes out, as from the bottom of a bruised heart, the lamenting cry, "Although my house be not so with God." Grey as an autumn evening ends the life of the great saint; of the man of love, of passion, of fervour, of inspired insight, of a woman's tenderness, and a hero's daring, and, above all, of a faith in God, so strong and deep that nothing in heaven, or earth, or hell could part him from his Lord. Grey it was as the autumn evening when, amidst the thickening mists and darkening shadows, he said to his beloved Solomon, "I go the way of all the earth," and then laid down his reverend head and slept with his fathers; but bright as the beauty of the morning shall be that resurrection day when he shall rise up after the likeness of his Son, and of his Saviour, and be satisfied with never-ending joy.

THE MAN OF GOD WHO CAME OUT OF JUDAH.

IT was a high day in that old town of Bethel. The great king of the ten tribes, the founder of the fresh dynasty which was to rival, if not to eclipse, the house of David, was present in this border town of his new dominion. To it, around his person, were gathered the chiefs of the families and the elders of the tribes. He was himself in person and in mind a born king of men. And those natural gifts had been improved to the uttermost by administrative experience, by foreign travel, and by his having drunk deep into the highest antiquities of the old world in its native Egyptian soil. Strange and wayward had been the vicissitudes of his life. He was of a stock which might have been suspected of hereditary hostility to the house of David from the return by Solomon upon the head of his old father, whom we know better as Shimei than as Nebat,* of the curses which he had heaped upon the great king in the time of his adversity. But he was yet of tender years when he was left fatherless, and had spent his youth in the house of his widowed mother, Zeruah, in Zereda of Ephraim. There he grew up strong, energetic, and diligent. He early attracted the attention of Solomon, and shared in his magnificent patronage. When that wise king, in the accomplishment of his vast architectural designs, was restoring the "Millo," which was, as it seems, the highest part of the old Jebusite fortress, which was now the city of David, Jeroboam was, amongst others, employed by him. The difficulty of the process evidently tested to the utmost all the engineering power which the king could command; and, as he watched the accomplishment of his purpose, and saw the breaches in the old wall repaired,

---

* St. Jerome identified Nebat with Shimei. 'Quest. Heb., 2 Reg. xvi., App. viii., vol. ii., p. 31.)

he noted in Jeroboam the faculties he loved to possess in a servant; he observed with pride his strength, his daring, and his untiring industry; and when the work of the Millo was finished he promoted his favourite to be ruler over all the charge of the house of Joseph—to be, that is, his chief officer in collecting the taxes and imposts due from the powerful tribe of Ephraim.

Promotion kindled the burning ambition of the young Benjamite. His charge over the house of Joseph made him feel the full amount of change from early vigour to a palsied feebleness which was passing upon the reign of the uxorious king, whose magnificence could not be supported except by imposts, the severity of which tried the loyalty of his people, and alienated them from the son of David. The transformation, too, of the nation under his influence from being a purely agricultural into a mercantile community, with the sudden enrichment of new families, and the free intercourse with foreigners which such a change entailed, was very unwelcome to the lovers of old customs, and generally offensive to the landowners. Even in the time of King David, the fickle temper of the people had more than once displayed itself; and a far less general discontent, when carefully cultivated by Absalom, had threatened his father's throne. The ill-humours of the time suggested to Jeroboam the possibility of a more successful revolt He multiplied his chariots and horses, and set himself at the head of a numerous band of followers. Nor was it without a higher sanction than his own ambitious longings that he thus began to "lift up his hand" against his master. He was meant by God to be the instrument of Solomon's chastisement when the heart of the aged king was "turned from the Lord God of Israel, which had appeared to him twice" (1 Kings xi. 9). Most unlooked for by Jeroboam must have been the granting to him of this high commission. He was not a man given to consort with prophets, or to listen to their words. But as he goes forth from Jerusalem pondering in his solitary walk his schemes of rebellion, Ahijah the Shilonite, the prophet of the Lord, meets him, and by sign and by word tells him that God will, for their sins, rend from the house of David in the time of the king's son ten of the twelve tribes, and give them as a kingdom to him. Into what a flame must such an announcement have stirred up his spirit! What a clear reading of all his secret desires did the prophet's words imply! "Thou shalt reign according to all thy soul desireth, and shalt be king over Israel." In that furious turbulence of his spirit it was hard for him to wait for the death of Solomon; and some indications of what was filling his soul would, in act or deed or preparation, find their vent. These were soon brought to the jealous ears of the old king, who, with something of his early vigour, sought to slay the threatening insurgent. Egypt was the natural protector of one in such peril—Egypt, the common home of expatriated leaders, the land which welcomed to its palaces all who would be the willing instruments of its crafty policy against bordering peoples. To Egypt Jeroboam fled, as Hadad of the seed royal of Edom had done before him. Like Hadad, if we may trust the

Septuagint, he was welcomed at the court of the Egyptian king, and given in marriage an Egyptian princess, sister of the queen, and of the wife of Hadad. In all this there was a large promise for the future; but there was much to stir up for the present the bitter waters of his soul. He was an exile at a foreign court; all the inevitable degradations of such a life chafed his imperious spirit. Time, too, was passing, and the old king lingered on still upon the throne he longed to seize. Such a life must have deepened all the hard lines of his stern character. Amidst the busy throngs of the Egyptian capital, through the gorgeous palaces of the Pharaohs, he moved as a shadow, with his heart afar off on the mountains of Canaan, buried in his own thoughts, forecasting his future reign, and weaving the dark threads of his lifelong conspiracy. Faith in the God of Israel, in the high sense of the word faith, his after history shows that he had none. The prophet's words were to him but as the promise of the Weird Sisters to the dark-souled Scottish chieftain, chanting back to him with a certain external authority the dreams of his own heart, and breeding within him a more confident resolution and more fixed purposes of daring. Instead of yielding himself submissively, like David, through his long years of adversity, and waiting to be the simple instrument of God's Will, his ambitious longings were even already a rebellion against God and a grieving of His Spirit; whilst the influence of the Egyptian mythology and creature worship, in the midst of which he found himself, obliterated any deep lines of exclusive faith in Jehovah, and prepared the way for his great after fall.

But at last the forty long years of the reign of Solomon were over, and news came down into Egypt that "he slept with his fathers, and was buried in the city of David his father." The dark heart of Jeroboam laughed with the gloomy joy of gratified ambition at the long-expected tidings, and he returned back to the old dwelling-place of Zereda, in the Mount of Ephraim, from which the jealousy of the old king had hunted him. Here he began to practise his former arts, and gathered round him all the tribe of Ephraim. The stupid obstinacy of Rehoboam helped forward mightily his projects. The oppressive tribute which Solomon had raised had shaken his great authority, and the dissatisfied tribes clamoured round the throne of the young king for a release from their burdens. Their reasonable cry was met with insult and threats, and the alienated tribes as one man looked abroad for another ruler. Then was the time of Jeroboam's triumph. He had put himself at the head of those who most eagerly demanded a reform of the abuses of the late reign. This gave him at once the position of a leader. His name was in all mouths. Stories of his exile, of his greatness in Egypt, of his return to his own people, of the magnificence of his life upon the Mount of Ephraim, of his wisdom, his strength, and his daring, ran through the ten revolted tribes; whispers as to the prophetic voice which long ago had destined him for the throne, seemed to add a Divine sanction to his usurpation. He was the very man they needed as their chief. We may see the working of his crafty hand in the great act of rebellion which consummated the revolt when the old chief of the tribute who had stood high amongst the princes of the wise Solomon was, as the king's representative, deliberately stoned to death by all Israel. After this act of rebellion return to the house of David was impossible, and all Israel made Jeroboam, the son of Nebat, their king.

Jeroboam soon showed that, however ready he might be to listen to the voice of prophecy when it promised him a throne, yet it was mere earthly ambition, and not the doing of God's will, which had been throughout his motive. When the promise of the kingdom had been made him there was joined to it a solemn charge to try his faithfulness. "It shall be," the prophet's word had said, "that if thou wilt hearken unto all that I command thee, and wilt walk in my ways, and do that which is right in my sight, to keep my statutes and my commandments as David my servant did, that I will be with thee and build thee a sure house, as I built for David, and will give Israel unto thee" (1 Kings xii. 38). It may well be that at the time visions of future service to God mingled themselves with the dreams of his young ambition. But the choking thorns had strangled the faint upgrowth of the better seed; and as soon as he had won the throne he set himself to keep it by his own subtlety, and not by obeying the God of Israel. The heart of the successful conspirator was darkened with the fear that if God's altar at Jerusalem continued to be the central point of the national worship, and was frequented yearly at the great feasts by all the males of his kingdom, the throne of Judah would supplant their unmatured affections to the throne of Samaria. "Then shall the heart of this people turn again unto their lord, even unto Rehoboam, king of Judah, and they shall kill me and go again unto Rehoboam" (1 Kings xii. 27). So much political craft his Egyptian sojourning had taught him. It had taught him also a remedy. His mind had shaken off the narrow trammels of the Jewish theology. The great impersonal Deity could, as he had come to think, be worshipped acceptably, not at one altar only, or only under one form. It was necessary to the strength and permanence of his dynasty that the new kingdom should have its own feature of national worship. If he could not impart to it all the hereditary sanctity of the altar at Jerusalem, he would at least emulate the splendour of the Jewish temple and exceed the gorgeousness of its ceremonial. He would interest in the service of the new sanctuary the great mass of his people. Instead of the sacerdotal exclusiveness which limited in Judah all the prizes of the priesthood to a single tribe, his enlarged mind would communicate them to all, and so enlist all in the maintenance of his new religious establishment. With the most engaging liberality he made priests of the lowest of the people. His keen eye discerned the sensuous tendency of his people, and he resolved boldly to reproduce amongst them the sacred emblems of the unseen God, which he had seen so deeply reverenced in Egypt, and he set up therefore at Dan and at Bethel the golden calves which should present sacramentally to his people the great Jehovah who had brought them up from Egypt. This was the very central point of his policy, and he devoted to its perfect establishment every resource he could command Bethel, no doubt, was chosen not only from its proximity to the dangerous border of the southern kingdom, but also from the holy associations which hung around it and made it so pre-eminently a hallowed spot. There the king had now gathered a crowd of obsequious worshippers. Tenderness for his people's needs was one great motive he assigned for the spiritual revolution he inaugurated. "It is too much for you to go up to Jerusalem : behold thy gods, O Israel, which brought thee up out of the land of Egypt" (1 Kings xii. 28). He was anxious to provide for them at a less cost than the journey to Jerusalem the full satisfaction of their religious desires. Nothing should be wanting which the king could command to make that supply sufficient. He made a house of high places; he multiplied beyond precedent the crowd of sacrificing priests—since as these were no longer limited to the tribe of Levi, he could fill abundantly their ranks. He appointed two great days of festival to rival those which were kept in the old capital. On the fifteenth day of the eighth month, "the day which he had devised out of his own heart" as an ordained feast for the children of Israel, all the magnificent ritual of the new temple was complete, and the great national worship was to be commenced. To add to the magnificent impressiveness of the scene, which was to remove from his people's minds any lingering recollections of the great Solomon's dedication festival of the temple on the mount Moriah, the king came down from his distant capital to attend the festival, and take part with his own royal hand in the service of inauguration—to offer upon the altar and to burn incense. It was impossible to overrate the importance of this occasion to himself and to his dynasty. If by that day's successful ceremonial he could thoroughly engraft upon the religious feelings of the people the new worship, his throne was safe for himself, and for his children after him. The dark heart of the long-practised conspirator concentrated its utmost energies to make this turning-point of all his long-laid and happily-accomplished schemes thoroughly successful. He had provided so far as the most anxious foresight would enable him against any possible failure, and now the crisis of the great experiment was come, and in the sight of all his people, "the king stood by the altar to burn incense."

We may picture to ourselves the whole scene: the band of supple courtiers; the new priesthood fiercely zealous in the assertion of their spiritual pre-eminence; the assenting crowd; pleased with their monarch's care; rejoicing in the bright promise of an external worship which met the longings of their carnal hearts; flattered with the distinction of rivalling or surpassing the worship of Jerusalem; with only here and there one whose grave, saddened countenance spoke of the inward struggle between the conflicting fears, on the one side, of dishonouring their fathers' jealous God, and, on the other, of incurring instant destruction if they opposed their fierce and strong-willed monarch. And now the king raises his arm to burn incense on the altar; when suddenly one unbidden presence intrudes itself within the inmost circle of his attendants. The garb of the stranger bespeaks him a prophet of Jehovah. The marks of travel are upon him; he has come from far; come, it may be, to take part in this grand service of initiation. One gaze, at least, rested full upon him. One master-eye was bent upon him, and sought to read in his countenance his unspoken message. What was the first emotion which throbbed through the dark heart of the anxious king when that unlooked-for figure first broke upon its consciousness? Had he come for good or for evil; to bless or to curse? Once before, with the same unbidden and unlooked-for suddenness such a form had stood beside him as he walked of old out of the highway of the city, had taken up the thread of his inmost thoughts, and forecast for him the strange future of his life. And now, with what message had this stranger come to-day? Was it the very same prophet, or one of the same prophetic line? What would be the burden of his prophecy? Self-flattery would whisper that it need not be unmitigably hostile. There was of necessity a certain rivalry between the prophetic order and the Levitical priesthood. The monarchy of the house of David had finally superseded the long line of prophetic rule; and the temple at Jerusalem had been a vast exaltation of the family of Aaron and of the house of Levi. Jeroboam's new temple and new hierarchy were the heaviest blow yet struck against the old Aaronic supremacy. Could it have been accepted? Might it be that prophetic lips would sanction his bold attempt to localise in his new kingdom and swell into hallowing devotion the waning worship of the distant tribes before this new altar to their fathers' God?

With these mingled other thoughts. Let his message be what it might, could he be mad enough to dare the monarch to his face? And yet could such an one, indeed, approve? And if he did not approve, why was he there, except he was sent by Israel's God to blast in the very agony of its birth the just-developed worship? We may see the eyes of the two men meet, and we can almost hear the deep hush which spread itself as a silence of hearts over the thronging mass around. What could come of it? Which would yield? Which wing would beat the other down? What would be the issue?

There was no sign of fear upon that prophet's brow. He stood as though he had already forecast within his heart all the scene before him, and was ready for its utmost need. And so, indeed, he was. When the divine afflatus had breathed upon him in peaceful Judah, it may be that the first impulse of his startled spirit had been to shrink aside from so infinite a daring. Jeroboam's strength of purpose, his unscrupulous employment of any means to reach his end, and his unflinching daring, were well known in Judah, and he was hated and feared as the despoiler of the house of David, and the divider of their nation's unity. To withstand such a man in the very central point of all his policy; to do it openly, publicly, without protection, in the sight of all his people, was indeed to cast his own life away upon an utterly hopeless hazard. But if human weakness had shuddered, God's strength had triumphed, and the messenger of Jehovah had girded himself to do the mighty bidding. As he walked forth alone along his appointed path, what tossing waves of conflicting emotions must have risen and surged within his soul! Even as he paced the streets of Jerusalem, the engrossing strife within had made him feel himself so utterly alone, that its crowded thoroughfares were to him as a desert. And now he had left behind him the outskirts of the chosen city; he had passed beyond the terraced vineyards with their walls and watch-towers, and was making his way along the high mountain ridge which formed the track to Bethel. From time to time he exchanged the white limestone path and the grey willow-like olive trees for the far distant views which that high ridge presented to his eye. He saw the border hills of Moab, girdled by the rich Jordan valley, where of old the threatening walls of Jericho had fallen at God's bidding before the trumpet blast of the circling host; and he thought upon the ancient charge, "Only be thou strong and very courageous," and built up his own spirit in the faithfulness of his God; or he looked upon his left and saw the blue sea brightly speckled with the ships of Tarshish, and swelling in its might under the breath of God; and he saw before him the outstretched rod of his prophet ancestor, and those waves at his command parting themselves asunder and standing as a wall on this side and on that, and his heart knew that he was safe in His hands who had divided the sea, whose waves roared and made the waters of the great deep to be a way for His ransomed to pass over. And now he was drawing near to Bethel; and as he thought upon his message, and there rose before his eyes all the abomination he was commissioned to rebuke, his soul burned within him from very jealousy for the honour of the Lord God of Israel. Was it not enough that, in distant Dan, where the Holy Land was passing into the unblessed forests of Bashan, the accursed altar should be raised, and the image of Israel's old sins be renewed, but must its presence pollute also the sacred grounds of Bethel, and insult the memories of Abraham and of Jacob? Must the very spot where, as he first trod the soil of the Land of Promise, Abraham had builded an altar unto the Lord and called upon the name of the Lord, see this forbidden worship rise to provoke Jehovah's wrath? Must the stones which Jacob had taken to be his pillow, when the great vision of God's nearness to him had been permitted to fill his wondering soul, be now builded into an altar to the calf of Egypt? Must the oak of weeping, which marked the grave of one of the great patriarch's household, now wave its branches over these unhallowed rites? The very trees of the forest which clothed the hill-side, as it stretched from Bethel to Ai, seemed, as they swayed under the breeze of the morning, to be uttering God's sentence on such daring unfaithfulness, and to lift up to the full comprehension of his message and the resolute determination to deliver it all the great soul of God's appointed messenger. With such thoughts burning within him, his feet trod the crowded thoroughfare; he passed through it as men pass through a city of the plague—he must touch nothing in it lest its pollution pass on him; he might not eat its bread or drink its water: by open sign as well as by spoken word, its guilt and desolation must be declared. And so with the foot of a resolute speed, he passed along its streets, trod the courts of the novel temple, passed through the self-opening circle of the idol-worshippers, and stood in threatening silence in the very presence of the haughty king.

But the silence was not long. Deliberately, and as one speaking in the ears of all, a sentence terrible to listen to, the denunciation was spoken. To the king, as though he were unworthy to receive it, no word was uttered. To the altar he addressed his words; upon the altar, the instrument and the witness of the monarch's sin, fell the terrible sentence. "He cried against the altar, in the word of the Lord, O altar, altar, upon thee shall a prince of the house of Judah offer the priests of the high places which burn incense upon thee. This is the sign which the Lord hath spoken: Behold, the altar shall be rent, and the ashes that are upon it shall be poured out." The pealing of the thunder-cloud could not have broken forth with a more startling burst. Every device of the cunning subtilty of the usurper was crushed beneath it. His scheme for a new national worship at the very moment of its perfecting fell helpless to the ground; here where he had hoped to raise a barrier against the weakening of his dynasty by any possible return of the brethren of the separation to Judah, here a Prince of the house of Judah should stand and burn the bodies of the priests of his new institution, to the power of whom he looked as the prolongers of the majesty of his royal race. Here on the very altar whereon he would consecrate his line, here should be the uttermost abomination of Hinnom, even the burning of the bones of the dead.

No wonder that his wrath broke forth—sharp, sudden, undisguised, unflinching. He might as soon abdicate his hardly won dominion as endure this intolerable ignominy. No sooner did he hear the words than he stretched forth with eager energy the hand which was about to burn the incense, and cried out, as though fearing the possible escape of the messenger of evil, "Lay hold on him." It was the action of a moment; but even as it was wrought, it was avenged. His hand which he had put forth against God's messenger dried up, so that he could not pull it in again to him; and the altar of incense—that too quivered beneath the word of power so that it rent asunder, and the ashes on it were poured forth.

The strife was over. God had, beyond all contradiction, put forth His might. The broken altar, the withered arm—these were the abiding tokens of the fray. The strong man of the earth had lifted up himself against the unearthly power, and it had shivered him to powder.

Calm, serene, unmoved, stood yet beside the altar the prophet of Jehovah : and as the trembling king entreats the prayer of God's servant for the healing of the arm which his word had withered, that stern strength in which his features had been set melted into mercy, and he besought the Lord, and the king's hand was restored to him again, and became as it was before. Humbled by the judgment, softened by the mercy, it seems for the moment as if that hard heart was yielding itself up to Grace—as if the hero daring of the man of God had rent, not only the altar-stones, but the harder rock of a rebellious spirit. "Come home with me," is now his utterance to the man of God, " and refresh thyself; and I will give thee a reward." Yet even this condescension is withheld. Those meats of the idol-worshipper were to be no food for the servant of the jealous God; Jeroboam's gold no guerdon for Jehovah's messenger. "The man of God said unto the king, If thou wilt give me half thine house, I will not go in with thee. Neither will I eat bread nor drink water in this place; for so was it charged me by the word of the Lord, Eat no bread nor drink water, nor turn again by the way that thou camest."

And so they parted: the king humbled, foiled, subdued; the fifteenth day of the eighth month —"the month which he had devised in his own heart"—marked as the day of his humiliation instead of his success; the great feast which was to have cemented the loyalty of Israel to his throne, having proved the first great shock to its stability. The prophet still, as ever, calm, determined, triumphant; spurning reward as he had laughed at threatening; and at God's command, turning from the guilty town by another way from that which had borne him thither.

How different were his thoughts as he left the

town from those with which he had entered it! The great burden which had been laid upon his soul had been lifted off. He had entered the town with a full sense of all that was before him He had cast himself into that eager and excited crowd of worshippers, knowing all the risk he ran: but not knowing what the Lord who sent him had appointed for him: he had obeyed simply, and he was victorious. He had been faithful unto death, and his Lord had stood by him and saved him.

What did that countenance speak as he left the evil town? Was it all thankfulness? Was there that sinking of the spirit which so besets humanity when it has accomplished a struggle which has tried it to the very uttermost? Or was there something of human triumph in the flushed cheek and bounding tread of him who had passed in through those gates pale that morning in the energy of subdued earnestness? It seems probable that these conflicting emotions were struggling within him. Struggling dangerously—foreboding, it may be, to the watchful eye of some guardian spirit all that followed.

What an unutterable sadness there is about that future! What lessons of self distrust, of the need of continual watchfulness, of the need of perseverance, woven in colours of blood into the bright web of his noble daring and high-souled triumphs!

He leaves the city, and as the first dangerous sign of yielding to temptation, he sits down to rest beneath a wayside tree, instead of pressing forward at any cost from the idols' home. But for that rest he might have triumphed to the end. For but for that the tempter, the old prophet of Bethel, would not have overtaken him and plied him with the falsehood which led to his signal downfall.

It is not difficult to trace the inducements which led to the utterance of that lie. The old prophet was one of those whose souls had once been visited by the visions of the Most High. But they seem to have vanished from him. Probably a life of worldly compliance had, as it is wont to do, dulled the receptive ear and made dumb the prophetic voice. His continued residence at Bethel, now that it had become the House of Idols instead of being the House of God, was an actual instance and for the future an unlimited promise of compliance with evil. In such an one, painfully conscious of the fading away of the prophetic power, there would of necessity be a craving for acknowledgment by a brother in the great company of the prophets, even for the satisfaction of his own uneasy conscience. Moreover, for his credit sake with others, he would desire to have the brotherhood avowed. The town was ringing with the fame of the nameless prophet—his calm courage, his unflinching utterance, the supernatural confirmation of his words, the yielding of the king, the high-minded rejection of the proffered present, the utter condemnation conveyed with such a terrible energy of expression in the refusal, on the command of God, to eat or drink within the accursed city—all invested the prophet-messenger with a marvellous halo of sanctity. That such an one should make no acknowledgment of the old prophet could not but lessen his already waning influence. What might it not effect in raising his reputation amongst his townsmen if the prophet who had rejected the hospitality of Jeroboam should be known to have been his guest? And so his scheme was laid: feigning, as such men learn to feign, what once had been real to him; utterly careless, as such old triflers with the voice of God evermore become, of the sin, and shame, and ruin which he might bring upon his victim, he sets out to overtake him and to bring him back. That halt under the way-side oak enabled him to fulfil his purpose. Doubtless the charge to return by another way from that which had borne him to Bethel conveyed to the awakened conscience of the prophet the charge to hasten far away from the sinful place, and so that halting was a tempting of God. Doubtless when the lie was uttered which was to lure him back, his conscience stirred within and warned him. But the temptation came in so seductive a shape—for old prophets counselling ease to kill the self-denying zeal of younger spirits, are ever Satan's chosen instruments of evil— it appealed with such an urgency of entreaty to his lower nature, for he was weary and faint, and the mid-day sun was hot and scorching, and Judea so distant, and present rest and refreshment were so needful, and he was in the unguardedness of spirit which is too often bred of recent success, and with something of the dangerous triumph of a great temptation mastered, and therefore of the right to some little self-allowance earned; and so he faltered and he fell. He who had received his own command direct from God, suffered it to be overborne by the word of a man, and he returned and ate of the forbidden bread and drank of the forbidden water. And even at the moment the voice of condemnation wakes against him, and the sentencer is sentenced, and the judge is judged.

Another man he set out upon that second return. No doubt the voice of judgment had woke up again his slumbering conscience. No doubt his very setting out from Bethel bespoke his reawakened faithfulness—he was in God's hands. Let Him do as seemed Him good. Bowed, humble, penitent, ashamed, he tracked the new path appointed for him. Its course led him by the mouth of the woody defiles which ran up from the Jordan valley to the central ridge—the wonted haunt of the wild beasts which breed there in the jungles of the river. From one of them comes the terrible roar, and the whirlwind spring of the avenger of his disobedience. To stamp unmistakably upon the whole act the character of judgment, the lion spares the beast which was his natural prey, and as though witnessing against the man of Judah, couches beside his lifeless form

Surely we must read in such a spectacle the glory and the risk of being the servant of the jealous God. The broken life, the dishonoured end, the strange sepulchre, the place amongst the catalogue of heroes, but the hero's name withheld, the escutcheon taken down, and the banner removed, all speak alike the undying lesson of not fainting in the battle, of not coming short in the trial; all echo the mingled threat and promise of the grand apocalyptic words, "Be thou faithful UNTO DEATH, and I will give thee the crown of life."

MICAIAH, THE SON OF IMLA.

IT is strictly in accordance with that system of correlation which is implied in the very notion of the government of the earth and all that dwell on it by an ever-present, ever-acting personal God, that great sins should call forth marked interference, and that great sinners should be met by great witnesses of God sent to withstand their evil deeds. All nature is full of material types of such a system of moral proportions. The vast plains of Africa abound with the large carnivora, and with countless tribes of all the larger ruminating animals. In the wild northern expanse of waters the huge cetacea have their home: as round the tops of the chiefest mountain-peaks may ever be seen the wide-winged flight of the great vultures and the sweep of the imperial eagles. The very rocks tell the same tale in their shadowy pictures of the melancholy wastes of those primæval times which followed first upon the chaos, and which stand before us full of the hideous and terrible tribe of Saurian monsters. This graduated scale in nature marks on the material world the impress of the same hand which, in His government of man, proportions the instruments of moral resistance to the instruments of sin.

It is not, therefore, in any sense surprising that, to meet so great a criminal as Ahab, other prophets of the Lord beside Elijah should from time to time have been raised up in Israel. For Ahab was indeed great in all the powers and proportions of his evil character. His influence over Jehoshaphat the king of Judah exhibits in striking colours his commanding nature. Scarcely any other king of Judah receives such commendation in the sacred record as is bestowed on Jehoshaphat, the son of Asa. He fortified his kingdom with widely-diffused garrisons. He furnished it with cities of store, to equalise in bad times the supply of food to its working classes: he established a system of national religious education, sending a royal commission, who "went about through all the cities of Judah and taught the people." He provided in it for the administration of justice; setting "judges in all the fenced cities," and giving them the remarkable charge, "Take heed what ye do; for ye judge not for man, but for the Lord, who is with you in the judgment; wherefore now let the fear of the Lord be before you: take heed and do it, for there is no iniquity with the Lord our God, nor respect of persons, nor taking of gifts. Deal courageously, and the Lord shall be with the good" (2 Chron. xix. 5—11). But, above all, he was a great reformer in religion; he "took away the high places and the groves out of Judah," which his father Asa, even in the first heat of his zealous restoration of the worship of Jehovah, had not dared to do. And in this great work he laboured by a personal progress through his kingdom, "for he went out through the people from Beersheba to Mount Ephraim, and brought them back unto the Lord God of their fathers" (2 Chron. xix. 4). Moreover, when trouble came upon the land from their heathen enemies, and the Moabites and the Ammonites came in "a great multitude" to invade Judah, he set his people the example of trusting, not to the wise military preparations he had so judiciously made, but to the arm of Jehovah. "He set himself to seek the Lord, and proclaimed a fast throughout all Judah." And such was his influence with his people for good, that at his call "they came out of all the cities to seek the Lord." And then, when God's prophet brought them a message of encouragement, "Jehoshaphat bowed his head with his face to the ground: and all Judah and all the inhabitants of Jerusalem fell before the Lord, worshipping the Lord." With the watchful wisdom which sought to seize on all favourable opportunities to promote the service of the Lord, he used this softening of their hearts to restore amongst them, with their own assent, and not as forcing it on them, that ritual of public thanksgiving which his great progenitor David had delighted to establish for the honour of his God. For, "when he had consulted with the people, he appointed singers unto the Lord, and that should praise the beauty of holiness" (2 Chron. xx. 21).

Such were his outward works. There was, moreover, behind them what gave them their deepest value, a true, earnest, personal faith in his God. "He sought to the Lord God of his fathers, and walked after His commandments, and not after the ways of Israel." Yea, so thoroughly did he so, that he is found worthy of the high praise, "He walked in the first ways of his father David, and his heart was lifted up in the ways of the Lord" (2 Chron. xvii. 3, 4, 6). Temporal prosperity followed largely on this devoted faithfulness. "He waxed great exceedingly. He built in Judah palaces: the men of war, mighty men, were in Jerusalem: and the fear of the Lord fell upon all the kingdoms of the lands that were round about Judah, so that they made no war on Jehoshaphat: and he had riches and honour in abundance." Such a man as this we might have expected to find visibly counteracting the influence and designs of the king of Israel, who had wholly sold himself to work iniquity, even though Jehoshaphat's wiser policy might have kept him from renewing with Ahab the war which, through all their days, had lasted "between Asa and Baasha, king of Israel." Yet, it would seem certain that he would in nothing mix himself up with the enemy of the God in whom he so sincerely trusted; and that he would use all his endeavours to keep his own family and his people free from the infection which familiar communications with the idolatrous court and nation would be so sure to spread amongst them. What a proof, then, of Ahab's power over others is given us in the startling contradiction of all such expectations which the actual facts exhibit! For, in immediate connection with the inspired statement of Jehoshaphat's abundant riches and honour, stands, in God's Word, the solemn note of condemnation, "And he joined affinity with Ahab." To such a degree did this power extend, which the naturally stronger mind exerted over the weaker, that it was not wholly swept away even by such words of terrible threatening as reached the king of Judah from the mouth of Jehu, the son of Hanani the seer, when, after the greatest perils of death, he "returned to his house in peace at Jerusalem," to hear, instead of the welcome which had so often greeted him from sacred lips, the startling reproach, "Shouldest thou help the ungodly, and love them that hate the Lord? therefore is wrath upon thee from the Lord."

Terrible in its consequences, even towards so favoured a servant of God, was the wrath kindled against him by this fellowship with the evil house of Ahab. It cost him the overthrow of that army he had formed so carefully, and with such success; it led to his navy being scattered, and his great "works broken of the Lord;" and it brought the sword, which followed the seed of Omri to destroy them, into his own house. For, first, that sword, in the hand of his own son Jehoram, cruelly and treacherously devoured all his younger children; then the Lord smote the murderer of his brethren with an incurable disease, of which he died miserably in his prime, leaving behind an evil name; "departing without being desired," and being borne to his lonely grave without honours; for "his people made no burning for him like the burning of his fathers, and they buried him not in the sepulchres of the kings." But this was not all, for the wrath reached on in the next generation to Jehoram's sons, with consequences of destruction, which are told with fearful plainness in the words of inspiration. "Ahaziah walked in the ways of the house of Ahab, for his mother was his counsellor to do wickedly. Wherefore he did evil in the sight of the Lord like the house of Ahab, for they were his counsellors after the death of his father to his destruction. And the destruction of Ahaziah was of God by coming to Joram; for when he was come, he went out with Jehoram against Jehu, the son of Nimshi, whom the Lord had appointed to cut off the house of Ahab. And it came to pass that when Jehu was executing judgment upon the house of Ahab, and found the princes of Judah, he slew them. And he sought Ahaziah, and they caught him (for he was hid in Samaria), and brought him to Jehu, and when they had slain him, they buried him." And even yet the sword ate on. For when Athaliah, the mother of Ahaziah, and his evil counsellor, saw that her son was dead, with the wild vengeance which lay ready to be aroused in the proud dark heart of the daughter of the Zidonian Jezebel, she arose, and with fiend-like cruelty destroyed, so far as she could, all the seed royal of the house of Judah. So far reaching in its issues of iniquity, so terribly remembered in its consequences of punishment, was the sinful subjugation of Jehoshaphat to the imperious will of Ahab.

It was not, we may readily conceive, without many resistances, though all too weak to stand the strong strain of temptation, without self-deceptions, ever ready to blind half-willing eyes, and remorse, bitter, but too late to be effectual, that Jehoshaphat yielded to the great but wicked king of Israel.

It is in the record of a signal example of this moral trial and failure of the good but over-mastered king that Micaiah, the son of Imla, first comes by name before us. The scene exhibits him as the witness for Jehovah, in one peculiar trial of his faithfulness, to which we have no record of Elijah's exposure, and without seeing which we cannot estimate at its full height the severe testing in those evil days of those who bore unflinchingly the burden of the Lord. We must have before us the whole scene, with what we know of the relation to each other of the kings of Israel and of Judah, to enter fully into the nobleness of Micaiah's grand bearing of his witness.

Jehoshaphat had been persuaded to go down and visit Ahab in that city of Samaria where, in open defiance of the God of Israel, he had set up for the worship of the court the statue of the obscene and abominable Baal. To come in friendly guise as the guest of such a court was of itself offence enough in one who feared the Lord. But according to its law of accursed fruitfulness sin ever follows sin; and one point of right yielded, is but the harbinger of the yielding of another; and so the king of Judah next consents on the enticement of his royal host to join him in a confederate attack upon the king of Syria. So far the evil influence triumphed unrebuked. Then succeeded one of those hesitating impulses bred of his better nature. As principal he would undertake no war without inquiry at the word of the Lord, nor engage in battle without "seeking the Lord God of his fathers." And so before the expedition was actually undertaken, he said to his royal compeer, "Inquire, I pray thee, at the word of the Lord to-day." It was easy for the king of Israel to yield a seeming compliance to what he doubtless deemed the hereditary weakness of his new ally: and with all the accidents of royal estate the two kings sat in a void place near to the gate of Samaria, "either of them on their throne, clothed with their robes," to hold solemn consultation with the oracles of God. The summons of the king brought at once before them four hundred prophets to declare the bidding of the Lord. A far larger number doubtless Samaria could easily have furnished, even after the destruction of the priests of Baal upon the mount of Carmel. For under its evil kings Israel had imported into the Holy Land all the idolatries of the heathen round them, and with each false god came an attendant troop of priests, and diviners, and soothsayers, and magicians. With such as these Elijah had contended in the solemn lists of the mountain of decision, and had triumphed over them openly. But it was not these idol-prophets whom Ahab would have called to remove the scruples of the good king of Judah. We may be sure that the four hundred who this day with one mouth declared good unto the king spake as spake Zedekiah, the son of Chenaanah, in the name of the Lord, whose word Jehoshaphat required. But he was not satisfied with the loud voice of the consenting chorus. So spake not at the court of Jerusalem the aged Hanani; nor with such semi-heathen tumults of utterance did his fathers' God reveal His Will through Jehu, the son of Hanani, and Jehaziel, the son of Zechariah. As one perplexed by the din of this artificial consent rather than convinced by its deceitful voice, the king of Judah asked, "Is there not here a prophet of the Lord beside, that we might inquire of him?" Ahab's keen discernment read at once, in all its causes and meaning, the secret dissatisfaction of the heart he desired to win, and he knew where to find the prophet, for whom, through all that surging number, the troubled glance of Jehoshaphat had searched in vain. But that man, for reasons of his own, Ahab would not willingly produce. "There is yet one man by whom we may inquire of the Lord; but I hate him, for he never prophesieth good of me, but always evil. The same is Micaiah, the son of Imla." Jehoshaphat's courteous disclaimer of such treason for the prophet, "Let not the king say so," was an irresistible demand of his presence; and an officer is sent to fetch him quickly. Then begins in all its severity the faithful prophet's trial. The officer who brings him tells him, as they hasten through the streets, the outline of all that has passed in that open space where in hushed expectancy the crowd await his arrival; he hears of the gathered company, the royal presences, the momentous issue, the concurring oracles, and that "the words of the prophets declare good unto the king with one assent;" and he is urged with friendly importunity, "Let thy word therefore, I pray thee, be like one of theirs, and speak that which is good."

From Ahab's words it is plain that this was not the first time these two men had met and measured their strength together. "He never prophesieth good concerning me, but always evil." What a sore, proud, revengeful, and yet crouching spirit the words betray! How gladly, but for the trembling of his spirit under an overmastering eye, would he have rid himself of those fearless, detested prophesyings! How plainly does the "I dare not" wait upon the "I would" of the conscience-stricken tyrant! How did he detest this intrusive prophet as such men ever do hate fearless reprovers! How far pleasanter to hear those voices prophesying good things with that glad accord! If only it were possible quite thoroughly to believe them! And now the king of Judah had uttered in outspoken syllables the voice which was murmuring already its dull, hollow sound to the sleepy conscience of the evil king; and he sends for this dark, unwelcome sayer of sad truths. When these prophecies of evil had been spoken by Micaiah the Bible does not tell us; but we have in this case no reason to distrust the statement of Josephus, that one instance of them is to be found in Holy Writ, although the prophet's name is not there recorded. It was, Josephus tells us, the son of Imla who administered to Ahab in his hour of victory over Benhadad that reproof from God, which must have been so inexpressibly galling to the proud and prosperous king.

There had been on that occasion a certain magnificence of triumph about his conduct. There was, first, the entire success of his arms against the mighty Syrian monarch, and then the seeming magnanimity of dismissing him in safety. And now the first was rudely wrested from him by the open declaration before his glittering staff that not his valour but God's judgment had subdued Benhadad; and then, for the second, his noble magnanimity is changed into his having disloyally allowed the escape of a great criminal committed by another to his keeping; and all this angry irritation is aggravated by his own sentence being unawares extorted from his unconscious lips: "So shall thy judgment be; thyself hast decided it." The severity of that sentence must have burned in its fiery sharpness into the very fibres of that angry and excited soul: "Because thou hast let go out of thy hand a man whom I appointed to utter destruction, therefore thy life shall go for his life, and thy people for his people." No wonder that the proud king "went to his house heavy and displeased." We can hear the echo of his growl of rage in the fierce outbreak to the king of Judah: "I hate him, for he never prophesieth good concerning me, but always evil."

With this scene before us, we can have no difficulty in believing further, what Josephus asserts, that the king's hatred had broken fort. in its natural expression by casting Micaiah into a dungeon; sooner or later under such a king the usual home of Jehovah's fearless witnesses. This account agrees entirely with the fact that Ahab knew, as he evidently did, where the prophet was; and was able to send at once for him, and command his presence, when "the king called an officer, and said, Hasten hither

Micaiah, the son of Imla." What a dungeon was in those hard old days, we read in the book of Jeremiah: "In the dungeon there was no water, but mire; so Jeremiah sunk in the mire" (Jer. xxxviii. 6). From some such dark and dreary tenement the prophet was drawn forth to stand before these kings. It seems as if his estate had touched the heart of the officer who brought him, and who, for very pity, besought him, "Let thy word, I pray thee, be like the word of one of them."

This was the special point of his trial. It was comparatively easy to stand against the prophets of Baal. In such an encounter, Jehovah was evidently with His faithful servant. It was the sham god against the true; it was the spirit of devils against the Spirit of the Lord. There was no room for choice: there was scarcely place for fear. Against such as these, though gathered against him by hundreds, Elijah had stood single-handed, and had triumphed openly. But Micaiah's trial was far subtler of approach, and so the more difficult to resist. These men professed themselves to be, even as he was, prophets of Jehovah. In His holy name they uttered their predictions. Probably as to many, if not all of them, there had been a time when the true voice visited them. In that peculiar dispensation the prophetic gift was the one only feature of the great Mosaic institutes of worship and communion with God, which remained to them. Altar, sacrifice, high priest, Urim and Thummim, the very law itself,—all were gone. There was left but these men on whom fell the afflatus of the Spirit, from whom yet breathed, now in whispers, and anon in thunders, the oracles of Jehovah. No one could foretell on whom the gift would fall. There were schools for those who sought the office, but not all of them were taken; whilst at His own will the free Spirit fell as upon Amos, who was neither a prophet nor the son of a prophet, but "a gatherer of sycamore fruit, a herdsman of Tekoah."

This gift, like all God's gifts, could, it seems plain, be turned by the receiver into evil. He might trifle with it; he might dumb its utterances through fear of man; he might pervert them for gifts and rewards. And as he thus trifled with the great power which had rested on him, he drove away its presence; and as the Holy One withdrew Himself, the evil one came near, "and entered in and dwelt there." He became a false prophet,—a prophet of lies. It may be that in the several utterances of the Spirit within him, he was at most but dimly conscious of the awful change which had passed upon him. The crisis of his moral trial had been accomplished when first, for fear or for gain, he tampered consciously with the truth; when he "divined for money." Now he was the victim of what then he chose. We read not so much of the false prophets prophesying consciously a lie as of their seeing lying visions, and so uttering deceits. As of old the vision spread itself before them in a dream, an ecstasy, or an inspiration, and what they saw they spoke. But it was a vision painted for them by the evil one; it was an inspiration bred of the low vapours of their own hearts, of their covetousness, their worldliness, or their greed. The next step in their evil course was the endeavouring by excitement, or even by forbidden arts of magic, to recall the ebbing power of prophecy. This darkening of the evil soul which once had known the light, is what Micah so awfully portrays, "Concerning the prophets that make my people err, that bite with their teeth, and cry, Peace. Therefore night shall be unto you, that ye shall not have a vision; and it shall be dark unto you, that ye shall not divine; and the sun shall go down over the prophets, and the day shall be dark over them" (Micah iii. 5, 6).

Yet it was only by the event that the falsehood of such prophecies could be determined, and he, therefore, who resolutely withstood them, took upon himself the risk of withstanding the true word of God. What it was which led Jehoshaphat, in distrust of those now gathered round him, to desire "a prophet of the Lord besides," we know not certainly. It may have been, as has been already suggested, the excitement of these professed possessors of Jehovah's Spirit. It may have been that he had heard of Micaiah in the dungeon, and that his heart turned sadly to the record of his father's sin in putting the seer into a prison house, and of the disease and death which, as God's chastisement, avenged that idle rage against the instrument of God's rebuke, and so, that the very fact of Micaiah's imprisonment for a faithful utterance, awoke within his soul an irresistible desire to test by such a witness the truth or hollowness of this consenting band of soothsayers. Great must have been the rage of these prophets of lies at this emphatic declaration of the king of Judah's distrust, eager their readiness to turn on him who was thus preferred before them.

Amongst this crew the single prophet stood. To him the dull stillness of the dungeon was suddenly exchanged for the eager interrogations of the king, the angry taunts of the prophets, the deep, expectant hum of the people. Instead of the darkened light and dreary outlines of the pit, in which he had been fed with "the bread of affliction and the water of affliction," there was the eastern sun, in all its glory, pouring down its rays on the splendour of the thrones of the two royally apparelled monarchs, and on the living sea of faces which filled the void space of Samaria. A feeble spirit might have been utterly dashed by the mere suddenness of the change—a weaker heart might have fainted under the heaviness of the burden laid so singly upon his solitary strength. But it was not so with him. Jehovah stood beside him, and he was not alone; he saw "the Lord sitting upon His throne, and all the host of heaven standing by Him on His right hand and on His left;" and the sun in its glory paled beneath that keener light, and the crowned kings, the crowding multitude, and the cursing and smiting prophets were as though they were not when set beside that grander company. Then the Spirit of the Lord fell on him, and found its utterance through him. This loud consenting chant of coming triumph was but the baseness of a mercenary lie. These prophets had prophesied for hire; and in counselling in Jehovah's name their counsel of deceit, had opened their hearts, and prostrated their intellects to the lying spirit. Their leader in iniquity, who had made him "horns of iron" for the misleading of his prince, and who had smitten God's true prophet on the cheek, should fly in vain from chamber to chamber from the avenging sword; the monarch on his throne of pride should be lured on to a defeat of ignominy and to a death of violence—he should come no more to his fathers' hill-crowning city in peace. Such was the word of Jehovah. Most bravely was it spoken; calmly, in the face of uttermost danger; resolutely, against all seeming improbabilities. The great warrior should be beaten down; the confederate kings should be overthrown; Israel, which had been taught to trust their own successful monarch as an unfailing conqueror, should be scattered upon the hill as sheep that have not a shepherd; nay, even the awful sentence of the great Elijah, should as it seemed be brought to nought; for how—if Ahab fell at Ramoth Gilead, three days' journey from Samaria—could the dogs lick his blood in the vineyard of Naboth, hard beside his palace home? Yet so the message was, and it was spoken out; a warning not to be listened to, but a prophecy to be fulfilled.

Yet a few hours more, and all was accomplished From that void space in the entrance of Samaria, the royal train rolled grandly back to the ivory house of Ahab; the company of prophets, whose voice of counsel had succeeded, swept triumphantly away; the gathered crowd melted and dispersed. The one man with whom was Jehovah's presence was led back dishonoured, smitten, and reviled, to eat the prison's bread and drink its water. The still night drew on, and all was hushed; the stars looked coldly down upon the silent square; angel bands guarded the dungeon prisoner; and he too, the day's tumult over, slept the sleep of peace. But the decree had gone forth, and "the watchers" were fulfilling it; and but a few days later on Gilead's mountains a king miserably dying, and an army slaughtered, scattered, and fugitive, attested the reality of Micaiah's mission and the verity of his words, "If thou return at all in peace, the Lord hath not sent me."

ELIJAH.

THE rise at all critical times of the world's history, of men eminently suited for the work they have to do, is a result, and therefore a proof, of the two great truths—(1.) That whilst the race of men, like other races of animals, is physically subject to the ordinary law of inherited life, yet that every soul is a separate creation, gifted, apart from all others, with its destined individuality; (2.) That the whole race is subject to a continually-acting superintending Providence. For, if there were no such individual differences, if all men, like the lower animals, were but passive representatives of the same idea,—as any one honey-bee is like every other honey-bee, gathers the same honey, makes the same cell in which to store it,—there could be no true kings of men. There might be in a man some instinctive power of gathering others round him, as there is a clustering of the swarm around its queen bee, but there could be no true kingship; no power in one man of directing or fashioning his generation by the intellectual, moral, or spiritual power which, as it is, his individuality enables him to exert over others. And again, if there were no superintending Providence governing the affairs of men, there would be no security for the right man appearing at the right time. Blind nature, not administered by a God, might produce a great poet when a great general was wanted; give a wonderful financier to a horde of savages, and set down upon the Stock Exchange the gallant, brave, and frank gentleman who could have wielded as a single soul a motley clan of Highlanders.

Now, instead of this unseasonableness of production, the world's history shows that the man the age needed has continually been given to the age. And, as we might expect, from the relation of the people of Israel to all other nations, this which profane history exhibits in its measure) is seen as in a pattern type in the history of the chosen people. Nowhere is this more distinctly traceable than in the life of the great prophet Elijah.

Sixty-five years had passed since the ten tribes had revolted from the house of David, and Jeroboam had mounted the vacant throne and reigned over them "according to all that his soul desired." Chequered years they had been: marked on the whole by much temporal prosperity, but clouded ever deeper and deeper with the dark shadows of spiritual evil. Jeroboam's reign began with all the vigour of a new dynasty; but ended in loss, disgrace, and untimely death. Abijah, the son of Rehoboam, though he "walked in all the sins of his father which he had done before him," and though "his heart was not perfect with the Lord his God," was yet as to power of mind and personal prowess a very different man from the feeble, boasting Rehoboam. He "set his battle in array with an army of valiant men of war;" he routed the force of the ten tribes. He "waxed mighty;" and he was wise in discourse as well as strong of arm; for "his ways and his sayings" were "written in the story of the prophet Iddo." He was the scourge of the usurper through all Jeroboam's later days. "Neither," is the sacred record of his chastisement, "did Jeroboam recover strength again in the days of Abijah; and the Lord struck him, and he died" (2 Chron. xiii. 20). The short reign of his son Nadab reached to but two uneventful years; that of Baasha, the son of Ahijah, who succeeded to the throne of the master against whom he had conspired, and whom he had smitten, lasted for twenty-four years, and was, through his "might," a time of military glory for the ten tribes. Baasha's provocations of the God who had "exalted him out of the dust, and made him a prince over Israel," brought extermination on his house and his supporters. His son was murdered after a feeble two years' reign, and the throne given by the army to Omri, the captain of the host. During his twelve years' reign, Omri bought the far-famed hill of Shemer, and built on it the city of Samaria; setting up there the throne of his dynasty.

There his son Ahab reigned after him for two-and-twenty years.

Ahab was what the world would call a great king. Its historians might describe him as taking up and carrying further the wise policy of the mighty Solomon. Instead of allowing his people to remain a mere agricultural or pastoral race, hemmed in by the narrow limits of their mountainous country, cultivating for themselves alone its rich valleys, and feeding only for themselves their cattle upon the upland slopes, he carried on the project which the wise king had formed, and had begun to accomplish, of making them a commercial people, and enriching them with the traffic of the earth. As Solomon had married the daughter of Pharaoh and formed a commercial treaty with Egypt, so did Ahab ally himself with the king of the Zidonians, intending, no doubt, to share with that queenly city the merchandise of the world. He made also for himself streets in the great trading capital of Damascus. Magnificence reigned throughout his days in Samaria; art was encouraged, and the increasing population better and more safely housed. In the book of the Chronicles of the kings of Israel is written the catalogue of the cities which he built, and the record of the ivory house which the success of his distant commerce enabled him to make. He was, too, successful in war, as well as great in the arts of peace. Twice he overthrew signally the forces of Benhadad; and recovered the cities which the forces of Syria had taken from his warlike predecessor, Baasha; and he fell as other brave men have fallen, in battle, heading an aggressive and invading army against the enemies of Israel.

But this worldly success was accompanied by an amount of wickedness unknown before even to the evil kings of the separated tribes. His father, Omri, the founder of the dynasty, had done so much "worse than all that were before him," that two hundred years afterwards the prophet Micah (vi. 16) set it before Israel as their special sin that "the statutes of Omri are kept." But worse even than that of Omri was the course of Ahab. "He did evil in the sight of the Lord above all that were before him; and as if it was a light thing for him to walk in the sins of Jeroboam, he went and served Baal, and worshipped him; and he raised up an altar for Baal, in the house of Baal which he had built in Samaria; and did more to provoke the Lord God of Israel to anger than all the kings of Israel that were before him" (1 Kings xvi. 30—33).

This introduction of the worship of Baal was a new and separate kind of sin from the iniquity of Jeroboam. His golden calves, abominable as they were, had themselves been intended to signify to a sensuous generation a local and special presence of their fathers' God. They were the instruments of a forbidden mode of worshipping Him; but still they were meant for His worship. What the temple at Jerusalem, with its altars, and its courts, and its sacrifice, was to the two tribes as God's special resting-place, that the golden calves of Bethel and of Dan, with their adapted ritual and their imitated priesthood, were to be to the ten. But to worship Baal was to introduce not only new rites, but a new god; to provoke Jehovah, not only by drawing nigh to Him with a self-invented and forbidden ritual, but audaciously to set up against Him another god. In Baal and in Ashtoreth, the great Phœnician male and female deities, were gathered up for the more polished tribes surrounding Israel the worship of the heathendom. Baal was, under different forms and appellations, the god of natural power, the god of light, the god of increase. Ashtoreth was the female corresponding deity. In many of these temples, in that of Baal-Peor especially, and generally in those of Ashtoreth, the rites of worship were defiled by the wildest sensual license; and all that could pollute and degrade humanity was practised in honour of these devil gods. It was this which Ahab had imported into Israel.

Nor was the establishment of this hideous worship all his sin. The Zidonian sharer of his bed and of his throne, whose very presence was a crime against the God of Israel, was not only zealous for the heathen god whose name her father bore, but, as a true daughter of Eth-Baal, was fierce against the rival honour of Jehovah. The great gift of prophecy, as though unwilling to withdraw itself, yet lingered with retiring footsteps amongst the separated tribes. God's grace, through the ministry of the prophets of the Lord, had still kept faithful to Him amidst the growing apostacy, seven thousand who were secretly faithful, whose knees had not bowed to Baal, and whose mouth had not kissed him. Against these prophets Jezebel had raged. It was not enough for her to maintain as her opposing spiritual army four hundred and fifty prophets of Baal and four hundred prophets of the grove, and to feed them as the chaplains of her house of idols at her own royal table, but beyond this she must exterminate the prophets of the God whom she hated. In her, as in other women of her class, under the painted cheek and tired head there lay concealed the cruel soul of the murderess; she "cut off" the prophets of the Lord, and would have destroyed them all if the courage of one who "feared the Lord greatly" had not, at the risk of his own life, hid the remnant in unsuspected caves, and fed them there with bread and water till the bloody days were passed.

In the full darkness of these evil days, the

bright light of Elijah's prophetic ministry breaks upon us in the sacred record with the startling suddenness of a meteor's blaze in the blackness of the night. Fatherless and motherless, with no record of his earlier days, with no hint of his training, he stands singly forth in a loneliness which is itself terrible. He is "Elijah the Tishbite, who was of the inhabitants of Gilead." From the recesses of that mountain land, nursed amidst its distant fastnesses, nourished by the bracing winds which swept over its lofty plateau; practised, as were all the Gadites by their border situation, and the frequent assaults of their neighbours, in all the resources, physical and intellectual, of the ever-watchful, ever-active Bedouin, he, a child of the desert, is, untracked, unexpected, and unwelcomed, suddenly, in the midst of the civilisation of Samaria and its court. At his first appearing, he is the stern threatener of judgment on the wicked king in the very height of his prosperity. He "said unto Ahab, As the Lord God of Israel liveth, before whom I stand, there shall not be dew nor rain these years, but according to my word." And the judgment announced, the prophet disappeared. It is like the flash of the lightning, sharp as a blazing sword in its sudden vividness; but not tarrying for a moment; revealing every thing, and gone as it reveals it. This first message is a sample of his whole ministry. To him was committed a dispensation of severity and judgment. All his meetings with the king bear the same impress. When the threatened judgment had run its course, and God's command to him is, "Go, show thyself unto Ahab," even in releasing the kingdom from its plague there is the same tone of severe rebuke. "Art thou he that troubleth Israel?" asks the king, with the peremptory challenge of one used, even in receiving favours, "to an absolute submission." The prophet who stands before the Lord answers him in words which must have broken with a strange ruggedness upon ears used only to courtly flattery, "I have not troubled Israel, but thou and thy father's house."

Once again the prophet and the monarch meet; and again it is with the suddenness, and almost with the crash of the thunder-bolt, that the presence of the man of God breaks upon the king's sight. Ahab has just triumphed signally in his wickedness. The obstinacy of Naboth had been overcome by his murder, and the king's heaviness of heart at being refused the vineyard which he coveted had been washed away in the blood of his liegeman. He rises up to take possession: he enters the longed-for fields: it is his own: his heart swells with the triumph. But what is that dark, threatening form, almost like the dead man's spirit? whose that voice heard before, and once heard never to be forgotten? The proud countenance of the earth king drops before the higher majesty. "Thus saith the Lord," is the terrible utterance, "Hast thou killed and also taken possession? In the place where dogs licked the blood of Naboth shall dogs lick thy blood, even thine." Ahab's answer, which comes back almost like the stifled growl of a crouching beast of prey, " Hast thou found me, O mine enemy?" only wakes up again the severe and unalterable sentence, "I have found thee, because thou hast sold thyself to work evil in the sight of the Lord. Behold, I will bring evil upon thee, and will take away thy posterity, and make thy house like the house of Jeroboam, the son of Nebat, and like the house of Baasha, the son of Ahijah, for the provocation wherewith thou hast provoked me to anger, and made Israel to sin; and the dogs shall eat Jezebel by the wall of Jezreel." For the time even that proud heart was humbled by the awfulness of the message, and the terrible severity of the messenger. And so they parted to meet no more.

Once again we read of the man of God standing in the presence of a king of Israel: and still it is with a like burden of threatening and of woe. Ahaziah had mounted his father's throne; and with his father's crown inherited his father's sins. "He did evil in the sight of the Lord, and walked in the way of his father, and in the way of his mother." He falls down through a lattice, and, suffering from consequent illness, sends to Baal Ekron to inquire concerning the issue of his sickness. God intercepts the message, and sends to answer it the man who was his father's terror.

The messengers return, not with the flattering

ambiguities with which, oracle-like, we may suppose that the priests of Baal would have allayed the fears and kindled the hopes of the heir of him who had made the worship of their god the religion of his court and people, but as men overawed and forced against their will to do the bidding of a mightier than themselves. They return with the strange tidings of their being met by one before whose imperious voice even the king's message had died in their mouths; by "a man who said unto us, Go turn again unto the king that sent you, and say unto him, Thus saith the Lord, Is it not because there is not a God in Israel that thou sendest to inquire of Baal-Zebub, the god of Ekron? Therefore thou shalt not come down from that bed on which thou art gone up, but shalt surely die" (2 Kings i. 6). Hereditary impulses of hatred and terror seize on the diseased king, and he asks eagerly of the messenger the lineaments of this daring interrupter of the royal embassy. The reply, that he was "a hairy man, and girt with a girdle of leather about his loins," is answer enough. It may well be that the Zidonian queen had stamped upon the imagination of her son those detested features; it may be that his words of doom, which waited twelve years for their accomplishment, kept alive within her breast a deadly hatred for their utterer. For three, perhaps four, years he had vanished from sight. Perchance he was dead; perhaps hidden amongst the mountains of Gilead, or buried in the caverns of Horeb. And now again, with a suddenness startling as of old, he stood beside them, again denouncing evil on the seed of Ahab. This time, at least, he shall not escape; and the captain of fifty with his fifty is sent to secure the lonely wanderer. The very number speaks the awe with which his wild strength and terrible vigour had impressed the court; and as it seems not in vain: for on the captain of fifty and his fifty, and on a second like company, the destroying fire falls from heaven. The third messenger, in humble guise, implores for himself and for his men mercy of the man of God, and is spared; and with them, on God's bidding, free and fearless, the prophet of the wilderness strides into the king's chamber, speaks again his sentence of dismay, and leaves it at his own will unfettered and unharmed.

There was no other meeting between the man of God and the house of Ahab: though, just before, or at this time, Jehoram, king of Judah, who had married Ahab's daughter and learned the customs of that evil house, received his fearful sentence in a "writing" couched in the stern sentences of the prophet of Gilead, "With a great plague will the Lord smite thy people, and thy children, and thy wives, and all thy goods" (2 Chron. xxi. 14).

Nor is it only with the royal house that the ministry of Elijah is thus marked as a dispensation of vengeance. By the priests of Jehovah's rival in His people's worship he is known as an unsparing avenger.

There is no dramatic record sublimer in its grand simplicity than the meeting of Israel and Elijah on the Mount Carmel. The World-God of nature and of strength is challenged before the assembled people to a trial with Jehovah. On Baal's side are the majesty of the crowned king, with his guards, his chariots, and his horses; the proud display of Jezebel's court and following, ready to maintain the cause of the heathen queen; her four hundred and fifty prophets of Baal, and her four hundred of Ashtoreth, with all their pomp of dress and elaborate ritual and innumerable victims and intensity of sensual devotion. Around them are the multitude of the people, the gathering of all Israel in ranks upon the mountain-side, watching with eager curiosity for that which is for ever to decide their halting opinion. In the midst of these cohorts of world prophets—gazed on with fear by the excited crowd, alone, silent, unmoved, obscure, like the dark mountain brow, wreathed with the thunder cloud—stands the prophet of Jehovah, with his rough and scanty clothing, his massive limbs, his untrimmed hair, as though witnessing for, and communing with, the invisible God, before whom their fathers had bowed. Throughout all the laborious preparations of the Baal prophets he is sternly silent, until he breaks in with awful irony upon their ineffectual incantations. And then when his turn is come, deliberately, and with careful accuracy, he builds up, as though with parabolic significance of what he knew to be his mission, Jehovah's long-ruined altar, and then that deep voice is heard by every ear, whilst it shakes every conscience, commercing with the Almighty. The fire of heaven attests its servant's truth; and with unsparing hand the prophet of the dispensation of severity himself, as it seems, puts to death the whole licentious crew who served in the polluted temples of Baal and of Ashtoreth.

But though Elijah's ministry was one of terror and severity, and though the aspect, garb, and habits of the prophet where all moulded into fitness for this special call, we shall altogether err if we picture him to ourselves as nothing more than a rock of the wilderness—a hard and obdurate avenger of iniquity. Such never are Jehovah's witnesses. Such never can, whatever terror they may strike, reach down into the depths of a nation's heart. It is in the union of these dark lineaments of massive strength and awful severity, with all the tenderness of a human heart, that the power of such a character consists.

And these are eminently combined in Elijah. What can be more touching than the almost woman's cry which breaks from that great soul over the dead son of the widow of Zarephath, "O Lord my God, hast Thou also brought evil upon the widow with whom I sojourn by slaying her son?" Is it not enough that I dwell a lonely man upon this populous earth, that no home voices ever break in on the stillness of my spirit's solitude, that no son ever clasps my knees, but that, for ever companionless, I bear Thy awful message; but must it be that my presence inflicts this loneliness on others? Is it not enough that I speak Thy threatenings to the obdurate? Must my dwelling in a house darken it with the shadow of death?

What an insight have we here into the deep tender sympathies of the prophet of severity!

How, again, does the same inner human heart reveal itself when he is driven of the Spirit into the wilderness of Sinai; when he sits down under the juniper tree and requests that he may die; when, the triumphs of Mount Carmel accomplished, the majesty of Jehovah avenged, the repentance of the people awakened, when he, the doer of these mighty works, finds out that he is not better than his fathers, cries for release from the long-borne burden of his loneliness—"I, even I, only am left!" What a relief it is, as we gaze on the stern rugged features of his giant daring, to see melt like the mists of the rising sun over the rock of the wilderness this haze of human gentleness around the otherwise almost Titanic features of his greatness!

It was doubtless by this matchless combination of the sternness of his prophetic dispensation with the inner tenderness of his spirit, that the wisdom of God fitted him for his peculiar work amongst the separated tribes. For that ministry he was moulded in the form of strength which stands before us at every turn of his mission; for that he was trained in the rocky mountain heights of his native Gilead; for that the rough sheep-skin mantle and the rude leathern girdle were the fittest dress; for that the long Nazarite locks of this (as the original has it) Lord of Hair hung down on his broad

z

shoulders; for that this mighty solitary spirit was taught to know a woman's clinging grasp and her heart-broken cry for sympathy and fellowship; for that in all the majesty of his strength he was lured into the silence of the desert and taught by the hurricane, the lightning, and the earthquake, that not in might, but in weakness; not in action, but in waiting; not in the battle cry or the shout of victory, but in the still small voice of childlike submission was manifest, the power, the presence, and the greatness of Jehovah.

What his mission was it may perhaps specially, at this day, be most profitable for us to trace. For amongst the ten tribes separated through their fathers' rebellion from the temple and its covenanted services at Jerusalem, all the various offices of the priesthood were gathered into the single person of the prophet. For this reason, as we might expect, it is in the ministry of the ten tribes, and not of the two, that the prophetic office finds its grandest development. Judah can nowhere show such men of God as Elijah and Elisha. And for what was this perfect instrument thus fashioned by the Spirit of the Lord? It was not to bring back the ten tribes to unity with the two. It does not seem that it was immediately to recall them to worship at Jerusalem. This might have lain behind as a hidden purpose of God's further mercy if the first call of prophecy had been received. But that first call was to an immediate purification of the life in which they found themselves, not to an exchange of it for another. That state was indeed the fruit of a past rebellion and an earlier sin; but it had grown to be their normal state, and as such, God accepted it. What he did call on them to do was to purify their existing state from the giant corruptions which had grown up within it. The Baal prophets must be slain; Baal worship must be rooted out; Jeroboam's golden calves must be ground into powder; Jehovah must be worshipped in sincerity and truth; and then He would open for them His further will. This, then, is the echo of Elijah's voice: Cast away the present sin, purify the system in which thou art from Baal and from Ashtoreth, from world worship, sensuality, and pride. Fall thou on this thy Carmel upon thy face, and let thy soul cry out, "The Lord, He is the God! The Lord, He is the God!" and thy spirit's drought shall leave thee, showers of grace refresh thee, heaven be open to thee. Live in this present life with God, and He, when it is His will, in His own time, will lead thee in other paths which thou knowest not, and set before thee, when thou hast been fitted to dwell within them, larger rooms of more perfect service.

ELISHA.

NO two men are linked together more closely in Scripture history than Elijah and Elisha, and no two are in character and the circumstances of their lives more sharply opposed to each other Elijah stands before us suddenly, without one note of preparation, in the fulness of the prophetic office as "the Tishbite, of the inhabitants of Gilead;" startling Ahab in his pride of power as though called by the king's sins out of the earth on which he stood; and denouncing judgment on him in the name of "the Lord God of Israel before whom I stand." We have no hint of the training for the prophet's office which preceded this its sudden development, though we may conjecture that his frame was hardened on the mountain ranges of Gilead, and his spirit attuned by solitary musings to the notes of power and judgment which marked all his prophetic utterances.

Elisha, on the contrary, comes before us with a touch of circumstance which almost reveals to us the history of his youth. He is "Elisha the son of Shaphat, of Abel-meholah." Instead of the child of the desert, full of the wild strength bred of lonely wanderings amidst the ranges of Gilead, we have the child of a peaceful, wealthy agricultural home in the rich valley of the Jordan. His call to the prophet's office finds him full of the employments which belonged to such a life. Elijah's homeward course from the marvels which had surrounded him at Horeb was ordered for him by the divine voice through the plain of Jordan. As he passes up it he reaches one of its pleasantest scenes, where the wood-tangled banks of Jordan, and the stern acacia groves open out into the rich arable plain, and the laughing brightness of a river-bordered meadow. He is at Abel-meholah, the "meadow of the dance," well known to the dark-eyed daughters of Judah and its jocund sons in festal seasons of rejoicing. There, on his father's lands, Elisha is superintending the ploughing of the fertile soil. The dark, awful form of the elder prophet rises suddenly on his view, and overshadows his soul with the mystery of a spirit's presence. He does not ask the errand on which the great messenger was bound; he does not venture to disturb the stride of that silent figure even with the congenial offer of an hospitable reception. But as Elijah passes by, still, as it seems, speechless, and as one borne onward by some divine impulse, he pauses for a moment, and the young man finds cast upon his own shoulders the well-known sheepskin mantle of the mighty Tishbite. Jehovah's call even in the doing of that simple act subdues his whole spirit, and he leaves the oxen and runs after the prophet, saying, "Let me, I pray thee, kiss my father and my mother, and I will follow thee." Elijah, with that deep knowledge of the springs of human conduct which is bred in solitary spirits by the introverted gaze so familiar to their souls, does but fix the hook in the already captive will of him whom he has mystically summoned, by the seeming disavowal of his act in the words, "Go back again, for what have I done unto thee?" Elisha's soul felt what he had done, and with no half-reverted, half-longing gaze after the sweetness of the home life which he knew was lost to him, but with the determination of a settled purpose which needed not to fly from enticements which he had already in his strong will subdued, he returns back from the departing prophet, slays for a parting feast of consecration the oxen whom he should guide no more along the furrows of the familiar plain, and then, having bid adieu to his father and his mother, arises, and goes after Elijah, and ministers to him.

Doubtless he forecast all, and it may be more than all, that this ministering implied; for it was not as a mere attendant servant, such as afterwards Gehazi was to himself, but as his fellow, and as his successor in his prophetic ministry, that Elisha was called by Elijah to leave all and to follow him. So the divine command had run, "Elisha the son of Shaphat, of Abel-meholah, shalt thou anoint to be prophet in thy room;" and so Elisha doubtless understood it. It needed no small share of courage and devotion to accept at his hands the fearful trust of such an office in degenerate Israel. What a life had Elijah's been! How must it have shown to Elisha in the very aspect of him who now stood before him, and mystically claimed his life's companionship! As that awful figure passed on its lonely way, what impression must have rested on the mind of the home-loving, happy son of Abel-meholah! In Elijah he saw what it was in Ahab's days to be the prophet of Jehovah. He followed with his gaze the houseless, homeless, saddened, solitary man, with his grand, deep, capacious brow, even at this moment darkened with the thunder of Horeb, with his uncombed Nazarite locks falling thick upon his shoulders, with his half-clad, great limbs exhibiting the gaunt strength of one conversant with hungry, droughty marches, with toilsome days and sleepless nights, with the defiant stride of one whose life was ever in his hand, threatened alike by the impulsive violence of Ahab, and the more dangerous, revengeful hatred of his Zidonian queen, and by the capricious impulses of a perverse people. But Jehovah's call brought with it Jehovah's strength, and he arose and ministered unto Elijah. So definite was Elisha's commission; so different even in its distinctness from the dark mystery which hangs around the unknown summons which had first compelled Elijah to bow his iron neck to the prophetic yoke.

Moreover, whereas Elijah's training is as untraceable as his call, we have at least the outline history of that of Elisha. He was known afterwards to one of the servants of Jehoshaphat the king of Israel as "the son of Shaphat which poured water on the hands of Elijah." For seven years at least the companionship and the training seems to have lasted; seven years which would stamp deeply on the receptive nature of the younger man many of the great outlines of the prophetic character of his master and his friend. And when at last he heard the fearful warning, "Knowest thou not that the

Lord will take thy master from thy head today?" and felt that he was henceforth to bear alone all the heavy burden of the prophet's office, we know as to Elisha the accompaniments as well as the fact of the full accomplishment of his call. The Spirit of God has recorded for us those unresting journeyings between Gilgal, Bethel, and Jericho, which preceded the ascent of the great Tishbite into heaven; the last communings of the departing prophet with his successor; the permission, "Ask what I shall do for thee before I be taken away from thee," in which, as though conscious of his approaching audience with the mighty Lord of all, he offers to send back from the heavenly treasury whatever his faithful follower might know himself to need; the "hard thing" which Elisha's craving soul desired—the double portion—the eldest son's inheritance—of his master's spirit; the doubtful grant of the bold petition, confirmed by the open vision of the ascension granted to his wondering eyes; the assumption of his master's mantle by the widowed successor; and the miraculous opening of his ministry, by the smiting and dividing with it of the Jordan waters.

This diversity in the providential training of the two prophets in some degree prepares us for the broad distinction stamped from the very first upon their prophetic course. Elijah's had been a dispensation of judgment; Elisha's was a dispensation of gentleness. Elijah enters on his office with the denunciation of the fearful drought, which for three years and six months consumed the land of Israel; Elisha opens his by healing at Jericho the spring of waters which were naught, and in their flow made the land barren: "So the waters were healed unto this day," says the sacred historian; and still tradition, reaching from Josephus to the reports of our latest oriental travellers, prolongs unto the present time the "this day" of the Bible chronicler. For still, above the present town breaks forth, on its north-western side, the healed spring, belting the arid plain with a band of verdure, and perpetuating to all time the remembrance of this pervading feature of Elisha's miracles. Such in character, with exceptions which shall be noticed presently, they were throughout. Thus, to run rapidly through them, he delivers the kings of Israel, Judah, and Edom from the destruction which lay before them in their campaign against Moab; he multiplies the supply of oil from the single barrel, which was the sole remaining property of the widow of the son of the prophets, whose two sons were about to be sold for debt; he obtains for the childless "great woman of Shunem" the coveted gift of a son, and, many years afterwards, miraculously restores him to life when the fatal stroke of the summer's sun had brought him to the grave; he heals the poisoned food, which threatened at Gilgal the lives of the company of the sons of the prophets; he multiplies the ears of corn to feed a needy crowd; he heals the leprosy of Naaman; he recovers the borrowed axe-head lost in the waters of the Jordan; and, finally, the very touch of his bones, in the tomb in which his body had been honourably laid, brings back its life to the corpse which had been thrust hastily deside his mouldering remains. It is not possible to mistake the character of this series of miracles. From first to last they bear upon them all the attributes of visitations of mercy. They are the very opposite of the judicial inflictions with which, through Elijah, the power of God broke forth to punish evil and to overawe the guilty.

Yet, as in the severe course of Elijah there is one touching scene of tenderness in the bringing back to life the son of the afflicted widow; so, as though to make the contrast complete, in the midst of the long list of Elisha's miracles of mercy there occur two miracles of startling judgment, absolutely needful, probably, in the evil days on which he was cast, for the assertion of his true prophetic character, and so for his fulfilment of the work which he was set to do. The first of them belongs to the early part of his career. Going, at the beginning of his long ministry, from Jericho to Mount Carmel, he passes through the town of Bethel; there, pre-eminently, the peculiar sin of Samaria had become inveterate, and had poisoned all the springs of reverence for Jehovah and His messengers. As he treads the hot ascent skirting the forest depths which had grown rankly over ruined Ai, the children of the idol worshippers, encouraged by their fathers' sin, if not by their fathers' actual presence, mocked the new representative of Jehovah's Majesty. They had trembled, it would seem, before the personal presence of the great Nazarite, and they ridiculed the smaller stature and more ordinary aspect of Elisha. "Go up, thou hair-cropped one, go up," was the taunt of those who might have seen with something of awe in Elijah the likeness of their mighty Samson. But the message of the Lord was not to be despised, and there fell upon the prophet the inspiration of judgment; and the curse which he pronounced on them, in the name of the Lord, was forthwith executed on the mockers by the savage denizens of the neighouring wood.

The other miracle of judgment seems dictated by a like necessity of protecting the ministry committed to him from falling into a dangerous contempt. It was the binding on Gehazi and his seed the leprosy of Naaman the Syrian.

Great had been Gehazi's sin; it had dishonoured the God of Israel, in the person of his prophet, by representing him to the Syrian stranger as taking rewards for the exercise of his superhuman power; it was, too, an absolute setting at nought the divine insight granted to his master in the attempt to palm off upon him a simple falsehood. Again, it was essential to vindicate God's honour that the punishment should be sharp, immediate, and patent to all. There was the same necessity as that which dictated the interruption of the gifts of life and healing, which signalised the apostolic miracles by the sudden destruction of Ananias and Sapphira, when they, too, in their day, lied in the person of St. Peter unto God the Holy Ghost. It was a note like that utterance of St. Peter against Simon Magus, "Thy money perish with thee."

But it was not only in the exercise of his miraculous gifts and the character of his miracles that this especial character of gentleness hung round the second great prophet of separated Israel, and distinguished him from his mighty predecessor. There is the same difference running through the whole recorded stream of his life. There is in Elisha no retiring into unknown and undiscoverable solitudes; there is none of that lightning-like presence and disappearance which marks everywhere Elijah's course. Elisha never dwelt in the lonely caverns of the range of Horeb; he is never fed by ravens in the bed of the mountain brook Cherith. His very garb bespeaks the difference between himself and the wild son of the mountains of Gilead. Instead of the scanty girdle and the sheepskin mantle, he wears the ordinary dress of those around him, so that, like them, in extreme sorrow he can "take hold of his own clothes and rend them in two pieces" (2 Kings ii. 12). He is the prophet of society, as Elijah was the prophet of solitude. He tarries with the sons of the prophets in their several haunts; he dwells in Jericho; nay, we find from incidental notices that he was possessed of a house of his own. For when, at his bidding, Naaman, the Syrian leper, is sent to him for the cure which the king of Israel had despairingly pronounced himself unable to procure, the great stranger comes "with his horses and his chariot, and stands at the door of the house of Elisha" (2 Kings v. 9). Another passage, too, suggests an inference as to the size of his dwelling, which seems to imply that the inheritance of the son of Shaphat had not been abandoned by the prophet Elisha, for we read that "Elisha sat in his house, and the elders sat with him" (2 Kings vi. 32). Nor was it only the elders whom his mansion was capacious enough to receive, for we find the king of Israel visiting him in it; and the direction, "Open the window eastward," marks, from its possessing such an instrument almost of luxury, the character of the dwelling-place. From these passing incidents, we may with certainty infer that, whilst Elijah was in the habits of his life the counterpart of the Arab of the desert, Elisha was the example of the civilised denizen of the town. And as he lives he dies. For him no fiery chariot waits. Like ordinary men he is "sick of the sickness whereof he dies." Round his death-bed friends gather; the king hears of his illness, and visits the departing prophet;

the slow progresses of gradual decay accomplish their work; he gathers up his feet into his bed, and dies; and his honoured body is interred in a marked and well-known tomb.

Without, indeed, a far more perfect knowledge than we possess of all the particulars of their own lives, and of what was passing round them, we may be unable accurately to ascertain all the reasons which required this striking diversity; yet some of the causes, perhaps, we may discover. The first great cause, doubtless, was one which may be traced everywhere, when we search deep enough to read the laws which are revealed concerning the hidden counsels of God in His dealing with His creatures. It is that law which Elijah, the prophet of visible power, so greatly needed to learn, and which he was taught in so marvellous a manner, when he stood alone with God on Horeb, when "behold, the Lord passed by, and a great and strong wind rent the mountains and brake in pieces the rocks before the Lord; but the Lord was **not** in the wind: and after the wind, an earthquake; but the Lord was not in the earthquake: and after the earthquake, a fire; but the Lord was not in the fire: and after the fire, a still small voice" (1 Kings xix. 11, 12). The crashing of the earthquake proclaims God's coming, but His presence is in the still small voice. It is the ever-recurring lesson, "Not by power, nor by might; but by my Spirit, saith the Lord." Elijah's mission was the mighty earthquake, Elisha's the still small voice. The one broke up the fallow ground and prepared the earth for the seed, yea, and sowed it often broadcast; but the other gathered in the harvest.

In many respects, moreover, we can see that the circumstances of the two differed widely, and required a corresponding difference in the Witness of Jehovah. Elijah had to defy in open fight, and make head against a great and successful king. Ahab and Jezebel, in their several spheres, were persons of strong will, of powerful minds, and of wide-spread popularity. They were the rocks which were to be broken in pieces before the Lord. Elijah's ministry, therefore, was of the temper of the whirlwind. Elisha lives, comparatively speaking, in the calm. Persecution was over. There was no more hiding of the Lord's prophets by fifties in the cave, to save them from the death to which a cruel queen had doomed them; and though the worship of Baal lingered on in the land, yet that heathen "lord of strength" had after the solemn trial on Mount Carmel, and the execution of his priests, been forced to retire into the groves, for the celebration of his rites, instead of openly proclaiming in the acknowledged worship of the court his triumph over Jehovah. To cope with such altered circumstances, Elisha's character was fitter than Elijah's. He could associate with the leaders of his own people; could influence society as only one who lives in the midst of it can; he could offer to "speak" for an applicant "to the king or to the captain of the host" (2 Kings iv. 13). He could visit Damascus not as the Bedouin of the desert, entering it suddenly, flashing out a word of fire, and then again leaving it as he came to find his safety amidst the untracked sands of the waste, before men had sufficiently recovered from the shock of his denunciations, to lay hands upon him; but as some great foreign potentate, on whom the general in chief would wait in solemn visitation, bringing with him "a present, even every good thing in Damascus, forty camels' burden" (2 Kings viii. 9), and to whom, as the representative of his sovereign, he could say with the reverential tone in which Oriental suppleness allowed the king of men to address the messenger of God, "THY SON Benhadad, king of Syria, hath sent me to thee, saying, Shall I recover of this disease?" (2 Kings viii. 9.)

Again, the schools of the sons of the prophets with whom lingered the true faith, and on whose safety and earnestness its maintenance mainly depended, needed for their support an Elisha rather than an Elijah. They required one who could live amongst them and raise their own habitual life, by the calm example and holy influence which distils dew-like round the man of God, in his ordinary life of devotion and obedience; and which could not have been given to them by the earthquake visitations of the terrible Nazarite.

We must not, however, associate any idea of

weakness with Elisha's character On the contrary, though there were more dramatic incidents of outward danger, and therefore more startling displays of courage and of strength in the career of his master; and though his desert life and wild ministry was of necessity fuller of picturesque lights and deep shadows, than that of the child of civilisation and society, yet Elisha's was really the more perilous life to lead. The double portion of the Tishbite's spirit was needed by him quite as much to uphold Jehovah's witness in the greater temptations to which his easier life exposed him, as it was to enable him to work the larger abundance of miracles which were requisite as credentials of the prophetic character in one living as an ordinary man amongst his fellow-men. It was comparatively natural for those who only saw Elijah suddenly emerge from his unknown dwelling-place, and by some terrible denunciations strike dismay into the heart of Ahab, and then retire again into the trackless haunt from which he had issued, to believe that he was the messenger of Him who had spoken to their fathers from the thick darkness amidst the thunders and the fires of Sinai. But to force upon them the conviction that one who lived amongst them, apparently just as they lived, was yet as truly Jehovah's witness, needed that perpetual display of more than human power which was so exceptionally exuberant in Elisha's ministry. And so for the inner life of his own soul greater visitations of the Divine Spirit were doubtless needed amidst the temptations of the court and the camp, and the town residence of Jericho and the country sojourning of Dothan, than when, as with Elijah, God and the soul were brought so awfully alone together, in the destitution of all outer things, amidst the savage scenes of the wilderness. But with all this difference there is no trace of weakness in the outline of Elisha's life and ministry. On the contrary, the sacred narrative seems studiously to record instances in which humanity, in all its strength, of fire, of tenderness, and of daring, breaks out amidst the tamer features which surround the more civilised man. Thus as examples: In the record of Elisha's great parallel miracle to that of Elijah, in raising to life the widow's son, there is a depth of tenderness which is not reached in the former history, touching as it is. The "great woman" of Shunem receives from the hot harvest field, with the cry of "My head, my head!" the son so marvellously given to her longing embrace. The boy sits upon her knees till noon, and then dies (2 Kings iv.). The bereaved Shunammite, with all an Eastern mother's love and inward resolution, speaks no word of sorrow; calmly tells her husband it shall be well, and mounts her ass, whilst with an eagerness which, for the first time, speaks an inward agony and purpose that will carry her through any toil, she bids her servant, "Drive and go forward; slack not thy riding for me except I bid thee." In the heat of her spirit she comes to the man of God to Mount Carmel. He, accustomed to her coming "at the new moon and the sabbath," as he worships amidst the shadows of the mountains, marks her distant approach, and waits for her until she comes to him on the hill-side, when she "caught him by the feet." Then comes that answer of

Elisha, which goes straight to every heart, as he reproached the servant who would have " thrust her away:" "Let her alone, for her soul is vexed within her, and the Lord hath hid it from me and hath not told me."

Again, what inward fire reveals itself as underlying the level outward crust of that calm character, in his words to the elders of Israel when King Jehoram sent to seize him,—"See how this son of a murderer hath sent to take away my head!" (2 Kings vi. 32.)

Again, what holy daring is there in his answer to Jehoram when he came in his extremity of distress from the forces of Moab to seek counsel of the prophet of the Lord,—"What have I to do with thee? Get thee to the prophets of thy father, and to the prophets of thy mother. As the Lord of hosts liveth before whom I stand, if it were not that I regarded the presence of Jehoshaphat, the king of Judah, I would not look to thee or see thee" (2 Kings iii. 13, 14).

It is well to note these indications of vast moral strength and purpose in Elisha, not only that we may form a true estimate of his actual character, but also to prepare us for considering the last reason to be here mentioned why one so different from Elijah may have been chosen as is successor.

From first to last, all holy Scripture is full of Christ. In direct prediction, in type, in example, He is ever re-appearing. It is the perpetual presence of this one master-figure, the marvel that throughout the ten thousand mysterious characters which are inscribed upon that still unrolling scroll the same image ever recurs, which, to the eye of faith, makes up the mighty wholeness of the prophetic record.

One great instance of such acted prediction appears in the succession of Elisha to Elijah. Our Master's own express words have, in a manner, identified the prophet of Gilead with the Baptist. The resemblance is most striking: the desert home, the austere fare, the awakening message, the sinking of each great heart under the overwhelming pressure of disappointment and rejection, the cry of Elijah under the juniper tree of the wilderness echoed in the message of John from the dungeon, the scantiness of Elijah's compared with Elisha's miracles, set side by side with the fact that John did no miracles; the one rebuking Ahab, the other Herod; the persecution of Elijah by the king of Israel, stirred up by his queen, driving him, as it were, for refuge to the fiery chariot,—that of John by Herod, stirred up by his brother Philip's wife, ending John's sufferings under the sword of the executioner, and sending him to his rest. Then, too, the unfinished work of each, left to be accomplished by his successor, stamp on each alike the marked description of "forerunner." Nor when we turn from Elijah to Elisha can we fail to see the figure of the Son of man mysteriously veiled beneath the outward aspect of the second prophet. For in Elisha's life in contrast with Elijah's is the very counterpart of that which tested and condemned the wilful unbelief of the scribes and Pharisees. "John came neither eating nor drinking, and they say, He hath a devil; the Son of man came eating and drinking, and they say, Behold a man gluttonous and a winebibber, a friend of publicans and sinners." Again, the solitary child of the desert was the forerunner of Him who sat at the Pharisee's table and lived in the house of Mary and of Martha. Again, there is the same contrast between the moral characteristics as between the accidents recorded of the forerunner and the follower in the history of the prophets of Israel, and in the records of the evangelists. There is the almost unrelieved severity of holiness of the one; there is its entire compassionateness in the other. In both cases the biting blasts of the desert proclaim their rude contrast to the soft breezes of Abel-meholah. There is the "Let her alone" of the prophet, when the servant would thrust away the woman who caught him by the feet; there is the "Let her alone" of the Lord when Mary anointed His feet and wiped them with her hair (John xii. 3—7). There is the weeping for the evils coming on the chosen people when Elisha read in Hazael's face the future woe, and when the Lord looked sadly on to the flight of the Roman eagle to Jerusalem. There are the sons of the prophets looking up in all things to their master; there are the twelve hanging on the Master's words, and St. John leaning on his breast. There is in the pitifulness of Elisha a faint human copy of the all-embracing tenderness which breathed in those words of wonder, "Come unto me, all ye that labour and are heavy laden, and I will give you rest."

Again, the resemblance between the special miracles of our blessed Lord and those of Elisha is most marked. For Elisha feeds with the few ears of corn the hungry multitude; he cleanses the leper; he raises the dead to life; he multiplies the oil for the widow of the sons of the prophets, and says, "Go sell the oil and pay the debt," as our Lord puts forth His power to enable Peter to pay the tribute money. Nay, even in the last recorded miracle wrought at his tomb, when the dead man about to be buried is, by reason of the sudden incursion of the invading bands of Moabites, thrust with precipitation into Elisha's tomb, and on touching the prophet's bones rises and stands upon his feet, we have in the far back ages a wonderful picture of every Christian man's death and rising again. For does not that caverned grave speak of the new tomb hewn in the rock wherein He lay who by death overcame death: who by lying in the grave brought into it for every one of us the light of heaven and the companionship of angels? Does it not speak of that reviving and standing on his feet which shall befall every one who by faith does indeed touch the Lord's body? and so is there not written as the interpretation of a miracle, the like of which is not to be found recorded in either Testaments, and which is at first sight startling from this singularity, as the legend of the whole life of the son of Shaphat, "Behold, a greater than Elisha is here?"

Nor is it only of the Lord in His own person of whom Elisha is thus a type. He foreshadowed in a most remarkable manner the Christ in His Church. "All the law and the prophets prophesied until John" (Matt. xi. 13). In him the old dispensation passed away. After him, as Elisha after Elijah, came the Son of God in the Kingdom of Heaven, the Christ in His Church; with the double portion of the Spirit; with far greater powers; doing "greater works;" with the Gospel gentleness instead of the thunders of the law; with the pervading universal influence from the gift of Pentecost which was to leaven all society and spread through all empires, instead of being the witness of a solitary people in the wilderness of the world to the unity of the Godhead.

Here is the last fulfilment of all that Elisha foreshadowed. No greater prophet than the mighty Tishbite had ever shaken the heart of Israel; yet his successor in the prophet's office received a double portion of his master's spirit; and so, whilst of the great Baptist it has been declared, "Amongst them that are born of women there hath not arisen a greater than John the Baptist," it is added, "Notwithstanding he that is least in the Kingdom of Heaven is greater than he" (Matt. xi. 11).

THE END.

PRINTED BY J. S. VIRTUE AND CO., LIMITED, CITY ROAD, LONDON.

www.ingramcontent.com/pod-product-compliance
Lightning Source LLC
Chambersburg PA
CBHW020301240426
43673CB00039B/672